A SACRED COMPASS

D1570302

A SACRED COMPASS

Navigating Life Through the Bardo Teachings

Anam Thubten

A Sacred Compass
Navigating Life Through the Bardo Teachings

©2020 Dharmata Foundation, Point Richmond, CA
First Edition

Credits:
Root Verses on the Bardo by Karma Lingpa, Reprinted by permission:
©Lotsawa House: lotsawahouse.org/tibetan-masters/karma-lingpa/
root-verses-six-bardos
Cover design by Anne McLellan

ISBN: 978-1-7320208-2-5

TABLE OF CONTENTS

AUTHOR'S PREFACE

Human life is a journey that goes through many twists and turns. Although we all belong to the same species, our experiences of life are utterly unique and individual. Various circumstances and our perspective on reality continually shape our life. Our stories of who we are have the power to create our very experience of this life on earth. In the end, our life is a human story that exists mainly in our mind, whereas animals seem to be living in the moment and don't carry the linear notion of their life woven by narratives that are always changing.

There are two ways to lead this life. One is to live unconsciously, going through all life's scenarios, without finding spiritual meaning in them, and responding to them from an unexamined conventional point of view or from our primitive proclivity. Another way to live is to bring reflection into everything and find meaning in all situations, responding from a higher state of consciousness, such as from love, compassion, and dignity.

Life on earth is short, and all the time that is gone cannot be recaptured. People might sometimes wish they could relive their life, that they could lead life as a wiser and even more enlightened being. But not even a single moment can be brought back once it has passed. Therefore, each moment should be treated as precious, and the state of mind we have at every moment matters. It is possible to lead life now and in the future more consciously, finding meaning in everything we go through and finding the highest freedom. Such a choice is ours. It is never too late to wake up and make that choice.

I hope that life is benevolent to everyone. In reality, everyone goes through ups and downs, and some people have to deal with tragedy. Yet there can be a silver lining even in struggles. Sometime, courage and compassion are developed through adversities. There is also the mystery of who we are and where we are going. We can prepare to embrace that mystery with courage, clarity, and insight, instead of with fear, confusion, and delusion. This is where the Tibetan Buddhist bardo teachings can be eye-opening for us. They can help us have the wisdom to navigate all the scenarios of life and show us how to work with difficult as well as existential issues.

The bardo teachings cover the whole range of life, from how to live to how to die. Since the Tibetan Book of the Dead was published in English in the early twentieth century, the Western world has become quite familiar with the bardo teachings. Even the word *bardo* is now a household word among certain groups and communities. The bardo teachings have often been written in quite archaic and traditional language. Yet they can benefit more people when they are expressed in practical and contemporary language. This is a task I took on, to the best of my ability and with good intention.

In 2019, I offered an online course on the six bardos, based on Karma Lingpa's work. After the course was completed, I thought about how to continue sharing these teachings with a wider audience, and the idea of writing this book was born. The transcription of the course became the basis of this book, with a lot of editing and additional new material. My friend Laura Duggan worked on this project tirelessly. I'm deeply thankful to her and to all those who supported me to complete this work.

Anam Thubten

Finding True North

STARTING OUT

The bardo is a very important part of our existence and even beyond. Buddhist masters, especially the Tantric Buddhist masters, developed extensive and profound teachings on the bardo. Let me explain a little bit about the bardo. Bardo is a Tibetan word, *bar do*. It literally means intermediate state, gap, or interval. It's the notion that you are stuck somewhere in the universe in an intermediate state.

People may associate bardo with a particular period of events within this life or between this life and the future. But in the ultimate sense, bardo refers to the cosmic period from the moment that our consciousness becomes deluded, trapped by the illusion of a separate self, to the moment that it wakes up, realizes there is no separate self, and knows that it is inseparable from everything. At that time, consciousness is utterly liberated, freed from its own self-manifested traps into what Dzogchen calls primordial purity, or in Tibetan, *ka dag* (W: *ka dag*).

Therefore, bardo can be interpreted in two ways. One meaning includes all the various stages, events, and periods in life, which have their own ups and downs. In the cosmic big picture, however, the bardo is our entire journey from being a separate self to the total dissolution of the separate self.

Being in the bardo means you haven't arrived at your destination. One analogy is when you are flying from one country to the next. You have left your home but you are not yet at your destination. That is a bardo. Another simple example is when you go to work every day. It is like a bardo when you are driving on the road, but you are not yet at your office. There are an inconceivable number of analogies we can use to describe the bardo as an intermediate state. In this in-between state, you have to cultivate reflection and other spiritual practices in order to not get lost and deluded. In that sense, the bardo is more than flying from one place to another. It is as if you are without a compass on some heroic expedition in a vast jungle filled with bellicose tribes and dangerous beasts. It can be perilous. You have to be alert and not be careless.

The bardo teachings are like a sacred compass. Like all the sacred teachings, they are reminding us not to get too attached to anything in this world—to where we are, to our life, or to the affairs in our life. "Don't get too attached to anything" is one of the main messages of the bardo teachings. They encourage us to be "in" the world but not "of" it, and they remind us that we don't belong to this world absolutely or eternally.

Where *do* we belong? We could say primordial purity. Yet this is not like a physical dimension, nor is it nothingness. It is something that is considered ineffable because words and concepts cannot explain it. Dzogchen masters often say there are things that cannot be fully explained by human logic. Logic only sees things as mutually exclusive, such as existence and nonexistence. Talking about the ineffable primordial purity, great Dzogchen master Jigme Lingpa said in one of his *dohas,* or songs of realization, "It is not existence because the Buddhas haven't seen it. But it is not non-existence because it is the all-pervasive ground of nirvana and samsara." He goes on to say,

> Taking sides on existence or nonexistence
>   completely collapses.
> Even Buddha's tongue gets stuck when
>   uttering this truth.

The teachings on the bardo are a very big part of my tradition and my own spiritual journey. Even though I have been teaching in the West, my roots are in Tibetan Buddhism. Everything I teach is based on what I have learned from the training that I received in Tibetan Buddhism. It's not that I came up with this treasure of spiritual teachings in Northern California while I was working in my garage, or that I am some kind of self-awakened guru who suddenly has so much to teach. Actually, I don't have any kind of self-awakening. Nothing really happened to my consciousness as far as I know. Most of the time, I am just using more contemporary language, logic, and terminology to teach what I have learned from my Buddhist training back in Tibet.

It feels like the right time to explore these extraordinary bardo teachings, which can open our hearts and change our fundamental perception of reality and who we are. In essence, the bardo teachings are not to be regarded as some kind of esoteric knowledge. Instead, they are very practical teachings that help us to live, die, and even continue consciously with awareness, courage, and love, not with fear, hatred, and delusion. Therefore, these bardo teachings are priceless.

The concept of the bardo can be found in the early Buddhist teachings, such as *Abhidharma*, which are the Buddhist texts that deal with cosmology, psychology, physics, and everything else in the world. The bardo is also found in the teachings of Mahayana as well as Vajrayana. Later, Dzogchen masters in the Nyingma lineage, such as Karma Lingpa from the fourteenth century, elaborated on the bardo teachings and took them to another level. These Dzogchen masters also famously taught the six bardos. The six bardos are the bardo of this life, the bardo of dreaming, the bardo of meditation, the bardo of dying, the bardo of dharmata, and the bardo of becoming.

Let me also invite all of you to not take these teachings as some kind of heavy Buddhist doctrine. This is not about acquiring a whole new doctrine. Anybody can apply these bardo teachings in everyday life as a sacred map to navigate life, which is full of both challenges and temptations.

To me, the bardo teachings invite us to open our minds toward the mystery of reality, life, and who we are. Sometimes we are stuck with very limited narratives about who we are and the nature of reality. Whereas life, the universe, our being, and our incarnation are so unfathomable that our minds cannot completely capture the full mystery. As human beings, we have a tendency to use our thinking mind, our rational mind, to come up with narratives and viewpoints that describe who we are, where we are from, where we are going, and what this life is all about. Then we get very attached to our narratives. This is how dogma begins. But to me, the bardo is not a dogma. It is an invitation to let go of our attachment to some of these narratives.

The bardo teachings are based on the notion of continuation. Is there continuation? Yes, there is continuation because if there weren't, we would not exist. There is continuation even though everything is illusion. But right now, there are a lot of narratives that may not accept the idea of continuation. One of the most powerful narratives in the modern world is materialism. Materialism is not just that people love a nice bathtub or worship their dashing-looking car or are attached to their physical comforts. It is more than that; it is an ideology that has been here for a very long time. This ideology has taken over the hearts and minds of so many people in the modern world to such an extent that we are denying a huge part of our existence—spirit, divinity, mystery, the unfathomable, and so forth. Our scientific, materialistic narrative about who we are tells us that we were born in a particular time, and that eventually we are going to die, which would be the absolute exhaustion or termination of our being, with no continuation.

This narrative also tells us we are just another mechanical entity, like a very intelligent and sophisticated robot that is made of flesh and bones, and has a complex nervous system. This view is fundamentally lacking in anything that is non-material, like notions of soul, consciousness, heart, or Buddhanature. Such a narrative can be quite depressing and partial. It doesn't capture the multiple dimensions of who we are. I think we human beings are more than just mechanical entities that are going to be terminated in the same way that material objects are terminated.

Although the materialistic narrative has its own logic and very convincing reasoning—it is very easy to completely worship it—the reality of our life is actually unfathomable. These bardo teachings invite all of us to open our mind and let go of our attachment to the materialistic narrative, and eventually realize that we are not who we think we are. Maybe we are something extraordinary, whatever you want to call it —pure consciousness, unborn awareness.

Recently I came across a photograph—though it looked like a black-and-white drawing—of our galaxy taken by the Hubble telescope, one of the largest telescopes invented. The picture is filled with dots. At first, I thought all the dots represented stars and planets. But the caption below said that each little dot represented a whole galaxy, which humbled me. At first, there was a little temptation in my heart to find out where I lived in that universe. But there was no way I could find the Northern California realm where I am living. Our galaxy was in the form of one little dot that has thousands and thousands, maybe even billions, of stars in it. Then I said to myself, "I'm going to put aside this futile exertion of trying to find my address or even find Northern California. How about if I just say I'm everywhere?" That gave me a big sense of relief. I felt maybe, after all, I am everywhere.

Of course, I am not referring to "I" as a personal self. But you see that if we can let go of, or rise above, our usual limited perception of who we are, we may be able to welcome and realize something extraordinary, miraculous, even immeasurable—in Tibetan, *sam gyi mi kyab* (W. *bsam gyis mi khyab*), the immeasurable or inconceivable nature of reality and who we are. Then automatically in such a moment of awakening, our delusion, our sense of separation between self and other, our hatred, our greed, all our *kleshas,* or inner poisons, might actually dissolve, at least for a moment. That is the power of such a realization.

Right now, many of us are walking on the spiritual path with the highest aspiration. Let me invite you to go inside, to feel and recognize the very impulse that motivated you to read these bardo teachings. This impulse is not just some fleeting or shallow impulse. It is an almost lifelong—or maybe even bigger than this life—deep desire, a longing to wake up and realize the nature of who you are, the nature of the universe, the nature of life, the nature of consciousness, and to be totally free, to be liberated.

Many people live unconsciously and really believe that the egoic version of who they are is their true nature. They believe all their life's affairs, they believe their personal identity, and they believe whatever is happening in their ordinary life. Yet somehow these same people feel that they are stuck. Somehow, they know that they are a prisoner of a kind of fundamental delusion or unawareness. Everybody feels that, even though people may not have that awareness all the time. I think deep down, everybody knows that we are stuck, we are dreaming, and we are not really seeing the true nature of who we are.

Therefore, there is a universal desire in all of us that wants to see a bigger reality, a reality that goes beyond self, goes beyond all our ideas, a reality that can wake us up, that can liberate us. People try to experience that liberation through science, philosophy, or spirituality. This is where our desire for transcendence comes into being. Such an impulse brought each of you to study these traditional teachings in order to ultimately wake up and see the bigger reality, to learn how to live and die in a more enlightened fashion.

Bardo Cycle of Teachings

The bardo teachings are elaborated in the Nyingma tradition, though other Tibetan Buddhist teachers and lineages have taught on the bardos. However, usually they talked about four bardos instead of six bardos.

In the Nyingma tradition, there are special forms of writing known as revelatory teachings, which are not considered written by the intellect but are considered inspired by visions or come from some enlightened dimension of one's consciousness. The people who write in such fashion are called *tertons* (W. *gter ston*), or treasure revealers. Karma Lingpa was one of them. Karma Lingpa, an extraordinary terton from the fourteenth century, revealed the complete cycle of teachings and meditative practices on the six bardos known as *zab chos zhi khro dgongs pa rang grol*, or *Self-Liberated Wisdom Mind*, which are attributed to the wisdom of Guru Padmasambhava. In addition to his writings, the ancient Buddhist tantras also contained quite extensive wisdom on the bardo. Karma Lingpa's teachings helped many people find a way to work with the bardos due to the freshness and clarity of his teachings. His teachings on the bardos are very rich and also practical. He provided many meditative techniques that we can use in order to bring about insight and wisdom in all the transitions we go through. We are using his *Root Verses on the Six Bardos* to open each bardo section in this book.

In the West, perhaps the first well-known Buddhist book was the *Tibetan Book of the Dead*, which was a translation of one segment of Karma Lingpa's teachings. The original translation was by someone who was not familiar with the tradition and therefore was filled with many errors and misunderstandings. But it must be forgiven because it was the formative stage for Westerners on the verge of discovering Tibetan tantric spirituality. Today, there are other accurate and scholarly translations available.

In general, many people understand bardo as an intermediate state after you die and before you take rebirth in different *lokas*, or worlds, a very specific period between the end of this life, this incarnation, and before your consciousness takes another form. This is one way many people understand bardo. However, many of the Dzogchen masters said that the bardo is from the moment you are deluded or separate from the primordial ground, *ye zhi*, until you go back to the primordial purity, *ka dag*. This means our whole life is actually a bardo until we become completely enlightened, until we return to the primordial purity, without having a chance to fall back into old habits.

So the bardo is very long. Sometimes people say, "I'm in the bardo." They mean, "I'm a little bit confused and lost." It is such a humbling thing to say "I am in the bardo." We have totally forgotten who we are, forgotten the nature of reality, so this is a giant bardo that is going nowhere, even though we think we are going somewhere. We are just circulating in this place called samsara, doing the same things—we get deluded, upset, or angry; we hurt each other intentionally and unintentionally.

On the other hand, the bardo is not always bad. There is a lot of wisdom, generosity, and kindness that happens every day. In the midst of the human condition, there is also so much beauty that we can appreciate. It is not a black-and-white picture; it is all happening simultaneously. And yet we generally do the same thing all the time. So everybody is in a bardo, as the Dzogchen Tantra teaches, until we are awakened, liberated in the primordial purity.

This is not my idea—this is taught in the Nyingma Tantras and by Nyingma masters. If we know that we are all in the bardo, then maybe we will have less attachment and be able to cut through our tendency to hold onto things as being very real and concrete. We may be able to look inside and see our own karmic neuroses, our kleshas, or inner poisons. Then we may have compassion and awareness in relation to our own delusion and suffering, and also view humanity with more compassion and understanding.

Nature of Mind

The fulcrum of all the bardo teachings is what is called "nature of mind"; in Tibetan, *sem nyid* (W. *sems nyid*). *Sem* refers to mind or consciousness; *nyid* means suchness or truth, the nature of something. *Sem nyid* is regarded as an already enlightened state of mind, one that is no longer bound by anything, including all human thoughts and emotions. Sometimes it is regarded as exalted and sublime. Other times it is regarded as the closest thing to you, something that you can have immediate access to. It is always at your disposal.

The world of mind and consciousness is not usually a favorite topic of conversation or even a part of our education. It is not often talked about or thought about, even though there is so much philosophy on the nature of mind that we can study. On the other hand, if we accumulate a lot of philosophical knowledge on the nature of mind, it becomes so cerebral that it doesn't do anything to impact our consciousness. Instead, we might just gain theories about it.

Yet this human consciousness or mind is extremely fascinating. It is like a cosmos in itself; there is so much to explore. The amazing thing about exploring consciousness is that we will begin to know who we are and the various roots of our experiences. The exploration of consciousness gives us wisdom, a means to be free from the limiting tendencies of the mind, and to experience something noble, which might be universal love, the ineffable, or even transcendence of self.

It is possible that our initial assumption about the mind or the nature of mind is that it is quite deluded and troubled, and it is not that enlightened. When we explore the mind itself, we see how restless and egocentric it is, and think this is the nature of mind. How could there be something profound under it?

Nature of mind really refers to the foundation or ground of one's own consciousness as well as its nature. Sometimes it might feel that the ground of consciousness is ego because the ego is so powerful and predominant, and we cannot imagine that we could experience freedom from it. The ego influences our experience every day. It's always calling the shots. It is hard to imagine there is another dimension of our consciousness other than the ego, or to believe that this ego is a transient perception or feeling.

Yet the ego is not permanent or inborn to us. If you are a meditator, this is obvious. For example, in the heart of meditation, inquiry, or sacred prayer, there are many moments when the ego somewhat dissolves, and a state of consciousness arises where there is no more ego. But even logically, it makes sense because there are so many moments in our everyday life pointing out that there is another state of our consciousness that is not egoic, especially when we forget ourselves and our problems. For example, walking alone in nature, you are struck by the silence or the beauty of nature, and then sometimes there is no more "you." You are gone. It is often easier to step outside of the usual ego-centered mind when we are immersed in nature. Whereas it is much easier to fall back into the egoic mind in the mundane world where everybody is walking around with a busy, restless mind run by the ego, a mind often filled with judgment, which then can enhance the same state of mind in each of us, as if it is contagious.

In Buddhism, the refuge ordination is when someone formally becomes a spiritual practitioner. She or he takes refuge in the three jewels: Buddha as a guide; the Dharma, or path, as the inner journey to freedom; and the Sangha, or the noble friendship. There are three main precepts associated with the three jewels. The essence of the last precept in modern language is, "Be careful who you hang out with." This is not meant to be taken literally. The point is not to allow ourselves to be easily influenced by the mental state of people in the world. When you are in nature, you are not in an environment that is trying to reinforce your ordinary mental activities or your mind's habits. The habits tend to subside, which reveals the transcendent state where the personal self or ego is no longer in charge. The transcendent state—deeply peaceful, serene, joyous, and full of love—reveals itself, because it is already there. Just like the sun shines when the clouds are blown away by the wind, because the sun has been there all along.

When we are born, obviously there is consciousness, but there is no conscious ego yet, only perhaps a tendency. As we grow, the ego develops, and the sense of separation begins to develop. Our identity and preferences are formed over time as we continuously evolve or morph. Ego is a mental game. The whole world is caught up in it. It is neither good nor bad—it is just how we exist as a species.

Then we have two tasks or two vocations. One is the earthly vocation that everybody needs in order to survive. In modern language, you have to get an education and know what you are going to do. If you have a family, you have to include their survival. And you may contribute to society by working and paying taxes. Then there is another vocation, the transcendent vocation, which would benefit us so much if we recognized its importance. But many people live and die without that recognition. There is a saying that some people were born but they never lived because they never did any inner reflection or practiced introspection, which is the transcendent vocation.

The object of the transcendent vocation is not particularly to survive but to experience or discover a deeper richness of existence, which might be universal love. The transcendent vocation also helps us not get trapped in the conventions of the world, which can be quite stifling. As long as we are trapped in the world's conventions, we are prisoners. There is nothing wrong with a life that doesn't have the transcendent vocation. Life continues with all its wonderful amenities and benefits. You could still have so much joy. You will find people you can love and a goal that you can be passionate about or work that you can offer yourself to. There is nothing wrong with that. On the other hand, such a life would be lacking some kind of awareness, and we would be living almost half-consciously because we would be trapped in conventions and delusions without even knowing it. This is why the philosopher Socrates said, "An unexamined life is not worth living." This was a radical statement. Ancient philosophers would often try to shock our mind and get our attention through radical statements like this. Yet through inner reflection, a whole new dimension of our life and consciousness is discovered. We can experience an egoless state of our consciousness where we are able to rise above our usual thoughts and feelings, our karmic patterns and our kleshas.

As human beings, we are a living paradox. On the one hand, there is an inherent goodness in each of us—our ability to love, to sacrifice ourselves for the benefit of others, and to act kindly. But this comes with other powerful forces and impulses, which can sometimes be quite dark, such as karmic patterns and kleshas. Karmic patterns are like mental or psychological habits that we all have simply from being in this human incarnation. Kleshas are sometimes quite destructive feelings and emotions that are part of evolution. Again, everyone has them by virtue of being human.

In Buddhism, there are five kleshas, also called inner poisons. They are called poisons because when we don't know how to handle them, they can be very toxic and destructive. The first three poisons, in Sanskrit, *lobha, dvesha,* and *moha,* are most often translated as greed, hatred, and ignorance. Then there are two others: pride and envy.

Greed, in Sanskrit *lobhah,* in Tibetan, *dö chak* (W.*'dod chags),* is a predominant mental and emotional state that runs through everybody's life. It is so present that we are very familiar with it and unfamiliar with transcending it. In English, we also translate it as attachment or desire. Almost every desire that arises in us belongs to the first klesha. Yet the translators didn't want to translate this klesha as desire but as greed. This is because we all understand that avoiding greed is wise, but desire doesn't seem so unwholesome. It doesn't seem like something that will corrupt our soul; for example, desire for chocolate, desire for comfort, or desire for companionship. There is nothing really wrong with these desires. If the senses didn't experience desire, it would be difficult to enjoy anything. But in general, almost any desire can bind us if we get lost in it. As long as we are not lost in it, then desire may not be so poisonous that we need to reject it. Otherwise, we would be living as some kind of ascetic, and we would have to practice some kind of austerity against everything that has to do with pleasure and enjoyment. This is not a direction that we want to take. Desire and sensual pleasure are fine if we are not caught up in them. So the first klesha is like being lost in desire.

But obviously greed is definitely poisonous because greed is a state of consciousness where we are already stuck and bound. The whole world knows greed is a vice. No one praises it. Much of our unhappiness is caused by some kind of greed, because we are attached to something or want more than we have. There is also all-pervasive greed on a larger scale. For example, we are all facing an ecological crisis that comes from greed. The corporations and capitalist institutions want to have more money, so they sometimes end up destroying the ecology and species. Our very survival is in danger. It all goes back to greed, people wanting more power, more territory. There is nothing good to say about greed.

The next poison is hatred, *dvesha* in Sanskrit, *zhedang* (W. *zhe sdang*) in Tibetan. Hatred also has different meanings. It can refer to pure blind hatred and also anger. Judgment and prejudice can be subtle forms of hatred. Hatred is based on ignorance and is a destructive emotion that has the intention to hurt or destroy the person or object to which it is directed.

Sometimes aversion can be a form of hatred. Aversion also does not exist outside ourselves, but is an experience that comes from seeing the whole world as a matrix of duality. Hatred is caused by feeling that one is separate from the rest of the world. It is very subjective, but when you don't know it is purely subjective, you project it onto a person or object, and basically end up hating the object. One of the best methods to set yourself free from this primal hatred is to own it as your projection. I think hatred is very dangerous when it gets out of control because it can cause one to hurt someone. We also don't want to develop hatred because we ourselves are the first victim of it; it takes away our inner peace.

The klesha of ignorance, *moha* in Sanskrit, is more subtle because the definition of ignorance is that, in a humorous way, you don't know when it is happening. This is why it is called ignorance. Ignorance can also easily turn into delusion. If you know you have delusion, you are no longer deluded. That's the interesting aspect of delusion. Delusion, or ignorance, basically has to do with all the projections, prejudice, and assumptions we have. On a coarse level, all our unhealthy belief systems are part of delusion, especially our projection and prejudice in relation to other people, which then cause so much disharmony. Many things that we are so clear about or that we believe—about our self, other people, or the world—are just mental constructs that take place in our own heads and often do not accord with the way things are. If we don't remember this, then we get really deluded. That's the bad news. The good news is that you won't be alone. You'll have lots of company, more than you want. Do you know the story about two patients who were having a conversation in a psychiatrist's waiting room? One said to the other, "Why are you here?" The second one answered, "I'm Napoleon, so the doctor told me to come here." The first patient was curious and asked, "How do you know that you're Napoleon?" The second one responded, "God told me I was." At this point, a third patient on the other side of the room shouted, "No, I did not!" Of course, this is just a joke, but there is so much delusion in the world. It would be even harder to live in this world if you were not deluded, unfortunately. You would be happy, but it would be harder because if you said what you saw, you would be unintentionally provoking everybody.

At a subtle level, delusion is quite rampant. Almost everything that arrives in our mind is a form of delusion. Delusion is really thick. Trying to wake up from it is like going against a powerful empire or trying to dismantle a giant, well-fortified edifice. Even the sense of self—the perception "I am separate from everything else"—is a subtle delusion. Yet in a moment of some sudden insight, even this sense of self becomes unreal. Many mystics or even great scientists state that this self is basically the ultimate delusion. Einstein said, "A human being is a spatially and temporally limited piece of the whole, what we call the Universe. He experiences himself and his feelings as separate from the rest, an optical illusion of his consciousness...."

Of course, it is not reasonable to expect that we will transcend every delusion in the world. We can go along with the consensus reality that is based on delusion as long as we are practicing *ahimsa*, non-violence. Even Buddha himself often said that he would go along with the world's conventions; he would not destroy them, even though many of them are illusory.

The klesha of pride is very interesting. Pride gives people a sense of being exalted and comes with a sense of being special. It boosts our ego. It can feel good for a while when you feel a lot of pride. Usually pride is based on delusion. You are comparing yourself with somebody else in your mind. Otherwise there wouldn't be any pride. People love and get addicted to the poisonous, toxic pleasure of pride because it makes them feel elevated. But because it is based on delusion, there is always insecurity even if we are not aware of it. There is fear. There is no pure blissful pride; it is non-existent. It is good to know this ahead of time. There is also very little love. It is very difficult to love and have authentic compassion when we are caught in the matrix of our own pride.

The fifth poison is envy. Envy and pride are very similar to each other. They both are based on delusion. Pride is thinking, "Oh, I'm better than that person," or "I have more this and that." Envy is feeling that you are less than somebody. Envy can be very painful because it brings up your own unkind feelings, judgments, and assumptions about yourself. It can trigger all your powerful psychological stuff like self-doubt and self-loathing. Sometimes we also want to destroy the object of our envy because of the pain it brings us. Sometimes people do quite crazy things, even hurt others, to release the painful experience of envy.

The inner poisons are definitely part of this human incarnation, and they give us a sense of being an individual, of being human. They give us a sense of life, too, where we can feel sadness, anger, confusion, and so on. If they are removed, what is life? Without them, it would be like trying to write Shakespeare without drama—it wouldn't be Shakespeare. At the same time, the kleshas can get really twisted and become destructive, to the extent that they can cause so much harm. So there needs to be a balance between accepting that we have these inner poisons and bringing enough awareness into our lives so that we are not governed by them. As we continue to grow inside, it is possible to let go of, or cut through, our identification with these inner poisons. On the other hand, when one becomes spiritual or a meditator, it is sometimes easy to develop dualism, thinking that all our humanness is intrinsically bad or unwholesome. We can even develop a sense of shame or feel bad about ourselves. This can cause a split inside, an internal holy war. So it is important to accept all our inner poisons as a part of evolution.

In the end, we are able to see that we are not even these kleshas. The great Indian Buddhist philosopher Dharmakirti said, "This mind is like clear light; the defilements are adventitious." In other words, the kleshas are temporary, and the nature of mind is not flawed. It is not bound by any of the human emotions or thought patterns. Therefore, we can go through transformation. If the nature of mind were flawed, we would not be able to change. This is the only good thing that one can say about all the poisons: they can be purified. They are not some kind of permanent characteristic of who we are; they are a karmic, mental makeup that can be changed. This gives us so much hope. The heart of spirituality and the bardo teachings is to look inside and see our own karma, our own habits, our own neurotic tendencies. If we are able to bring the light of awareness to them and begin to let them go, then we will have a much more meaningful and even happier life, and the world will benefit from us.

In the *Uttaratantra,* Acharya Asanga depicted the nature of mind by describing the layers of consciousness in the context of ancient Buddhist cosmology. This cosmology states that in the beginning there is just space. In that space, the element of air comes into being, which becomes the force that creates the foundation or ground for the world to exist. Upon the air, the element of water forms. Upon that, the earth is formed and the world comes into being. Similarly, Acharya Asanga said, the experience of reality we have, including the samsaric aggregates or faculties, depends on karma and kleshas. Karma and kleshas depend on delusion. Delusion depends on nature of mind. In the same way that space is the foundation of all the elements, the nature of mind, or Buddha mind, is the foundation of everything. Also, just as space depends on nothing, so the nature of mind depends on nothing else. The nature of mind or consciousness is the basis of everything. Acharya Asanga's verses say,

> Delusion has its basis in the mind's purity whereas the
> true nature of mind has no basis in any
> phenomena.
> The nature of mind is like the element of space—it
> has no base and no abiding.

This is a very positive, sacred psychology due to its assertion that the very fundamental characteristic of our consciousness or mind is intrinsically enlightened and wholesome. It is also pointing out that we are not just the body or the elements or the faculties, which are a "mixed bag" since they carry a lot of karmic patterns. Our own body is a miraculous vehicle because through it, we can exist and feel we are alive. We can enjoy all the delights of sensation, pleasure, eating food, and so on. Without our body, we couldn't experience all that. But our body can have pain, be exhausted, and also carry a large amount of unfinished, evolutionary, generationally-transmitted memories, pain, and trauma. So it is a mixed bag. Here Acharya Asanga is saying we are more than any of that. We are something utterly pure.

The ancient masters knew the nature of mind. They were the best scientists of consciousness. Like the astronauts who spend their whole lifetime exploring the cosmos, the masters explored consciousness. They called the nature of mind by many names—original mind, Buddha mind, *tathagatagarbha*, pure consciousness, pure awareness, primordial ground, and so forth.

While the nature of mind is always present, it is often obscured by kleshas. Therefore, the ancient masters devised techniques to experience it, such as tantric initiations, various yogic disciplines, and meditations such as koans. According to Dzogchen, the technique is really simple. It is so simple that you either get it or you miss it. It is good when something is so simple. We like things to be simple, but then if we miss it, it is so difficult. When something is complicated, we can chew on it and figure it out. Then we can say, "I'm on the way to understanding it." It feels good, like we are getting somewhere. But when something is subtle, it can drive us crazy, especially if we don't know what it is about. There is nothing to chew on. We can't tell ourselves a nice story, such as "I am on the way." When it is so simple, its subtlety can elude us.

In Dzogchen, the method to experience nature of mind is almost like no method. Often Dzogchen talks about the "three unmovables." Unmovable means not to do anything. Just relax.

The first unmovable is called unmovable body. This means resting with the body relaxed in a comfortable posture and holding the mudra of resting in the nature of mind. This mudra is just relaxing your hands face down on your thighs. The mudra reminds you not to struggle but to rest in the nature of your own mind, which is already enlightened. Nothing very effortful. You make sure that your back is straight to let the energy flow easily and to feel still and dignified.

The second unmovable is unmovable faculty. You are not trying to control your faculties, such as ears, nose, or eyes. You just relax, and you don't try to control the senses. Just let everything arise—sounds, sights, colors, shapes just arise.

The third unmovable is called the unmovable nature of mind. This means you do not do anything with your mind. You are not trying to meditate, to fix or alter your mind, or to get somewhere. You are not rejecting some experiences or holding onto others. Drop all the effort, as if you are doing nothing. Your mind will not go utterly blank, even though there is no more effort of thinking, imagining, or conceptualizing. A natural awareness is revealed, which can see, hear, taste, and feel. That natural awareness just happens when you are totally relaxed. It is not an effect of any cause. Yet everything else continues to unfold—the world outside and also the world within, the world of thoughts, emotions, moods, and physical sensations. As you just sit without doing anything, you welcome what might arise in your natural awareness without identifying with any of them. Resting in that natural awareness, there is a possibility that if you are totally ready, if your heart and mind are open, you will experience the nature of mind, which is totally free from your ego and your kleshas.

This is unbelievably simple. It happens all the time to meditators. As you practice these simple methods, you know how to drop into that state of mind where everything is clear. All your problems and struggles go away, and the whole reality becomes very clear, illuminated. Without trying to invoke anything, the best part of yourself is revealed, which can be love and everything you aspire to in the realm of human goodness.

Once there is an authentic experience of the nature of mind, then various simple methods can be applied to wake up your mind and reconnect with the nature of mind. Often, we do not abide in the nature of mind; thoughts, opinions, and emotions constantly bombard us, trapping us every day. Then we become deluded or we suffer. This happens quite often while we are not meditating, but it can also happen while we are meditating. In the Tantric Buddhist literature and liturgies, the syllable *phat* is mentioned. In the Dzogchen tradition, meditators periodically shout this syllable as loud as they can, so that it almost shakes their body and basically shakes their mind. Then their whole train of thought stops right there. Yet it is not like going into some kind of sleepy, unconscious, or blissful meditative state. Instead, it has the opposite effect. It makes you feel very alive. Your senses are open, and your mind becomes sharp in that moment. At the same time, whatever train of thought you were on is gone. Phat takes you away from whatever state of mind you might be stuck with. For example, a thought that caused you to worry is gone in that moment. It is like you are starting your whole reality from a fresh ground. This method is often used by Dzogchen masters. They exclaim this syllable in daily life to refresh their mind and go back to the nature of mind for a moment.

These kinds of techniques are not unique to Dzogchen. Somehow human beings have figured out methods to get out of the mind and be in touch with a place of freedom inside. One time in the city of Seoul, South Korea, a few people were riding with me to the hall where the weekend meditation retreat was happening. The woman who gave me a ride said that when she was young, now and then she would worry and be quite upset. Then she would stuff herself with chili sauce. It was so hot that it burned her whole body, and her train of thought stopped right there. She had found her own method to find inner freedom. Shouting *Phat!* is a lot easier in that sense.

Pointing-Out Instruction

Usually in the Dzogchen tradition, and perhaps other traditions too, everybody has to go through a long preparation before they receive the teaching known as the pointing-out instruction or *ngotred* (W: *ngo sprod*). This is a method through which somebody can point out your true nature to you, point out truly who you are. Someone can point out the nature of consciousness, the nature of your being, your original face. Or they can point out what you are not—that you are not the ego, you are not the self, you are not your suffering, you are not your karma. The pointing-out instruction is like introducing you to the nature of mind the way somebody directly introduces you to someone else.

The idea is that somebody can cut through all the words and concepts and instead point out "that," whatever "that" might be: the unconditioned, emptiness, original face, the ineffable, or no-self. Imagine, for example, there is some kind of exotic fruit that you have never eaten. But you read a lot of books about it and have a great deal of information. You can imagine the color and flavor, but you never actually tasted it. You might even have ample information to write a book about it. The idea with ngotred is that somebody does not waste your time. They just pick up the exotic fruit and say, "Eat it." Then you eat it, and you can say, "Okay, now I know what that fruit is."

Traditionally in the old days, a master would give the pointing-out instruction, ngotred, one on one or in a very small gathering. The skillful master would lead someone through a simple meditation guidance to experience nature of mind on the spot. Sometimes their methods could be improvisational. Once the famous Dzogchen master Nyoshul Lungtok Tenpé Nyima became a very close friend and student of the great Tibetan master, Patrul Rinpoche. Patrul Rinpoche was known for always being very humble. Nyoshul Lungtok asked Patrul Rinpoche on a number of occasions to give him the ngotred, because he felt he hadn't really understood the nature of mind experientially. But Patrul Rinpoche didn't respond to his request for a very long time. One evening, they were camping outside in the mountains.

Suddenly Patrul Rinpoche said, "Do you remember you asked me to give you ngotred?"

Nyoshul Lungtok said "Yes."

Patrul Rinpoche said, "This is the time for me to offer that to you."

Then without any rituals, prayers, or anything else, Patrul Rinpoche asked Nyoshul Lungtok to lay down on the ground on his back. Then Patrul Rinpoche asked him,

"Do you see the sky? Do you see the stars and the moon?"

Nyoshul Lungtok said, "Yes."

"Do you hear the dogs barking in the distance? Do you hear that I'm talking?"

Nyoshul Lungtok said "Yes."

Patrul Rinpoche said, "That's it. That's the nature of mind."

At that moment, Nyoshul Lungtok had a profound epiphany where he felt he realized the nature of mind. Even though this sounds so simple, it makes sense, because in that moment, he had dropped all his mental activities—past, future, judgement, worry, and so on. He was fully in the present moment, in direct touch with reality in that moment. So it makes sense that the profound awakening happened to him with such a simple method, through such simple communication with Patrul Rinpoche.

I had the chance to receive pointing-out instructions a few times. The last time was from Lama Garwang, when he was still alive. He was one of the older lamas, an extraordinary Dzogchen master from old Tibet. These old lamas are very authentic and kind of enlightened in many ways. They have transcended almost everything. They are extremely innocent and pure. I don't think many of them exist now, except maybe one or two in Tibet. I miss these older lamas very much.

I felt that I needed the pointing-out instruction again, and I wanted to make sure I received these precious teachings from an authentic teacher. So I sent a monk to Lama Garwang to request ngotred, the pointing-out instruction, from him. There was a little bit of excitement but also a little bit of worry that he might refuse my request. Sometimes the teacher refuses your request and your ego can make up a lot of stories, so I had both excitement and fear. The monk came back and said, "Lama Garwang said he is happy to offer you the pointing-out instruction. He said you can come to see him tomorrow." I was very happy to hear that and became like a little innocent child who can't wait for New Year's or Christmas eve. I had some ideas about what magic might happen, some preconceived ideas of what it would be like, some amazing enlightenment inside me. The next day we went to see him.

Lama Garwang was sitting on his bed. In the old days, many people used their bed as a sofa during the day, sitting on it, and then at night, they would sleep in their bed. Their bed was everything for them, which is quite convenient. Lama Garwang was sitting on one of those traditional square-shaped beds.

I bowed to him and said, "I am so happy that you are going to offer me the pointing-out instruction. I'm so thankful to you." As part of the tradition, I bowed to him three times and recited prayers as a ceremonial form of requesting these precious teachings from a master. Then he said a very few words. One phrase was "awareness without a trace." He went into silence and then said, "That's it." That was the end of the ngotred. The whole thing didn't take very long. I bowed, thanked him, and left. Part of me was enthralled that one of my deepest wishes was fulfilled that day.

"Awareness without a trace" is an important phrase that is used in the Dzogchen tradition. It is a state of awareness that is not stuck with anything. Just as when a bird flies in the sky, it doesn't leave any kind of trace, in the same way, all the thoughts arise and are self-liberated, and don't leave any trace behind. They arise but because you are not holding onto them, they dissolve. That's the analogy. Awareness itself also doesn't leave any trace, as it is free from grasping at thoughts and experiences, and is not attached to itself either.

After I left Lama Garwang's house, I kept going back in my mind, trying to re-examine what happened. What happened? It was very hard for my mind to capture any content because there wasn't anything where I could say, "Oh, that is what I experienced." My mind couldn't say I experienced bliss, universal love, or saw some kind of lights. There wasn't anything my mind could capture. When I reexamined it, I saw that Lama Garwang was trying to point out a state of mind that was unbelievably simple, a state of mind where there was not so much ego. It is so easy to miss it because it is really subtle. Our mind tends to look for something sublime, fantastic, or spectacular in those occasions. But it is so subtle. There is nothing that should be happening other than relaxing in the ordinary state of mind. When you are relaxed, all the egoic tendencies dissolve. There isn't anybody there. But it is so easy to overlook. This is why his few words and his unassuming, simple instruction were directly pointing out the nature of mind. Because the nature of mind is subtle, the teaching is also subtle.

But this is such a boring experience to the ego. The ego wants to be somebody, right? The ego wants to be anybody so long as it is not nobody. That is what ego doesn't want. The ego wants to be a devil or Buddha, it doesn't really matter which, as long as it becomes somebody. But what it doesn't want to be is nobody. It doesn't want to become nothing. That is very scary for the ego.

Basically, in that moment, my mind was quiet, with only a few thoughts here and there. It sounds so ordinary. I do not want to give any name to that state of mind. But now I have a new relationship to that experience.

When you are experiencing the nature of mind, the three mental states—attachment, hatred, and delusion—are gone, dissolved. The ego stops. It is more about what is not happening than what is happening. Our mind tends to understand things by what is happening. But the experience of the nature of mind is very subtle and can be understood by realizing what is not happening. This is very liberating even though it is not very exciting to the mind. Once you become familiar with that state of mind, it becomes very rich and profound.

I think if we are open, our true nature is always revealing itself in some moments. During meditation instructions, when you are concentrating, suddenly somebody says, "Now let go of all your effort or your concentration. Allow yourself to drop as much as you can. Drop effortlessly into what they call the natural state of your mind." If you pay attention, maybe you have become pure awareness—you are no longer the ego or you are no longer identifying yourself as the ego. Suddenly you are free for a moment, you are free from everything for a moment—free from your karma, free from your suffering, free from your pain. That is also a moment when you can experience your true nature.

Sometimes it happens quite easily during a loving-kindness meditation such as the four immeasurables: immeasurable compassion, love, joy, and equanimity. You may think, "Oh, this is only a loving-kindness meditation," but there is something very profound happening even though it is packaged very simply. When we practice the four immeasurables, we are invited to drop into our heart and feel that our heart is courageous, pure, and selfless. Our heart has the ability to hold everything. The whole experience is no longer mental. It is very physical, experiential, visceral. If you pay attention, if you just notice what is happening, maybe you are no longer actually identifying with the ego, the self. Maybe in that very moment you are truly who you are, which is nameless. You can call it the primordial Buddha, egolessness, or the tathagatagarbha.

When you are going through the usual challenges in everyday life or are in any of the bardos of living or dying, the answer for all of the challenges is to relax in the nature of mind. Then everything is clear. Confusion turns into clarity and the mind stops feeding its own misery. It stops right there. You are left with pure inner liberation regardless of what is unfolding on the outside.

When you go through the bardos, each bardo presents some kind of test for you: fear, confusion, or being lost. If you remember to go back inside and drop into the nature of mind, then all the internal conflicts go away right there. You transcend the bardo, and you are no longer stuck anywhere.

PART I:
BARDO OF THIS LIFE

ཀྱེ་མ༔ བདག་ལ་སྐྱེ་གནས་བར་དོ་འཆར་དུས་འདིར༔
ཚེ་ལ་ལོང་མེད་ལེ་ལོ་སྤངས་བྱས་ནས༔
ཐོས་བསམ་སྒོམ་གསུམ་མ་ཡེངས་ལམ་ལ་འཇུག༔
སྣང་སེམས་ལམ་སྒྱུར་སྐུ་གསུམ་མངོན་གྱུར་བྱ༔
མི་ལུས་ལན་གཅིག་ཐོབ་པའི་དུས་ཚོད་འདིར༔
ཡེངས་མ་ལམ་ལ་སྒྱོད་པའི་དུས་ཚོད་མིན༔

Kyema! Now when the bardo of this life appears,
Life has no spare time so I will abandon laziness,
Enter the path of study, reflection, and meditation,
without distraction;
Take perceptions and mind as the path,
and actualize the three kāyas.
Now that for once I have attained a human body,
This is not the time to live obliviously.

BARDO OF THIS LIFE

Now let's look at the first bardo, the bardo of this life, *kyé né bar do* (W. *skye gnas bar do*) in Tibetan. The bardo of this life is from the moment you are born until the moment you die, until you have gone through the process of dying. But this is a very rough description. Right now, we are in the bardo of this life. "This life" is the life that you are already experiencing. But this life is quite illusory too, even though we may sometimes think it is so real. It seems as if it is continuously going to unfold. When you hear the term "this life," what might your response be? Our response often depends on what we are going through. We don't always think of our life as the period from birth to death. Instead we think of our life as what we are experiencing at any given time. Sometimes we have total love of this life and sometimes we really don't like this life. Have you ever had that experience?

For example, let's say you go to the beach somewhere in Northern California when it is not too foggy. You make sure that you take some snacks or something to eat. You may walk with your friends during the beautiful sunset, then take off your shoes and walk on the beach. Maybe you listen to music, or if you don't listen to music, you just sing some songs in your heart and watch the sunset. Then you may feel, "This life is extraordinary. I do not want to be anywhere other than where I am."

Of course, this is an exaggerated example, but sometimes things are going well in your life. You just paid your phone bill. Then somebody wrote you a beautiful letter, or someone may have sent you a gift, a beautiful flower, or a poem. Or you just came out of a nice shower or a two-hour bath, and there is gourmet food waiting for you, or maybe there are wonderful friends or companions waiting for you. You think, "Yeah, this life is actually pretty good. If anybody can teach immortality, I want to be the first person to learn that esoteric knowledge. I want to live here."

But then we go through a lot of changes in our experience of this life. Sometimes life is very hard or difficult, and things are falling apart; you go through trauma and tragedy. I heard a Buddhist teacher say that he is not afraid of death, but he is afraid of life. I hope this is not something that we are always experiencing. I wish that we always had the feeling that life is not something we have to be afraid of. But sometimes life can be very challenging, especially when we are struck by trauma and tragedy, which unfortunately exist in this human world.

When we focus on what is happening in the immediate period, we have a hard time capturing or envisioning life from an all-encompassing viewpoint, as a whole journey. Yet in general, life is relatively long. Buddhism talks about the four rivers of existence: birth, old age, illness, and death, which are cycles that every human being goes through. These cycles are a powerful part of reality. They illustrate that life is a relatively long journey in which people go through different stages. These cycles are like rivers that are too powerful to go against.

Either you happily swim or white-water raft along with them, or you struggle against them.

Sometimes people may feel this human life is *too* long, especially if there is no more meaning or magic. Such a feeling does not strike us often because each day there are many moments that are ordinary yet beautiful, where the grace of existence washes all the disappointment or boredom away and allows us to feel pure joy. It could be catching the sight of a sunset, seeing the smile of your friends, having a cup of tea, or overhearing your neighbor playing *bossa nova* music. Yet sometimes things can become too ordinary, and everything becomes so familiar. You feel you are doing the same thing again and again all the time, like the movie *Groundhog Day.* One time after a meditation retreat, a circle of friends got together, and we invited each other to talk about our own *dukkha (Pali)*, which is a Buddhist term for suffering. Its connotation is that everyone suffers, whether to a great degree or in a subtle way. One of my friends, who is retired, is a very good person, and as far as I know, no major tragedy has happened to her. I was curious to know what her dukkha would be. She said, "Well, I don't really have so much suffering but periodically I feel the drudgery of everyday life, not finding magic in life or in the moment." My friend is a very good meditator. I know that even when such feelings arise, she knows what to do with them. But imagine if someone didn't know what to do with that feeling. They could really feel life is too long.

There is a little town a few kilometers from the town in Eastern Tibet where I grew up. One family in that village was good friends of my family. They often invited us to eat. The food was very simple, and there was not that much to eat—barley flour with butter and, if you were lucky, milk tea. The wife's sister was a woman who went blind and I remember she wasn't very happy. From that time on, I had a fear of blindness. As children, we would think of the worst things that could happen and for me, it was going blind. I felt that would be so hellish. We have all these ideas about what can truly ignite joy in us and what can destroy it, ideas based on unfounded assumptions. Yet even if something terrible happens, like blindness, if you are in the right state of mind, life can have magic. Helen Keller was one of my heroines, an inspiring figure for me. She became blind and deaf at an early age, yet became an inspiration to humanity. She once said, "The best and most beautiful things in the world cannot be seen or even touched—they must be felt with the heart." Someone who is blind can be in touch with the beautiful things in life. They can be in touch with joy.

On the other hand, life is really short. There is so much uncertainty in life that many people do not go through the full life laid out in the ancient maps. Unfortunately, some people never have the chance to experience old age. They may die as infants or when they are young. Often young people die from terminal illness, accidents, or various other catalysts. Life is on such flimsy ground that we can be struck by unexpected tragedy at any time.

Even if you have faced all the stages of life, it is still very short. As Buddhist teachers often say, cherish this life. This is also taught by Western philosophers. For example, the Roman emperor Marcus Aurelius said, "When you arise in the morning, think of what a precious privilege it is to be alive— to breathe, to think, to enjoy, to love." He also advised people "...to know that a limit has been set to your time. Use every moment wisely to perceive your inner refulgence or it will be gone and nevermore within your reach."

Path of the Bodhisattva

Buddhism is quite advanced, not only regarding its understanding of the nature of consciousness but also the nature of the universe and the cosmos. Buddhism teaches that there are many *lokas* or worlds, many galaxies, and countless universes, and among all the galaxies, our world is the most interesting realm. It is called *sahaloka* in Sanskrit, and *mi jé kyi jigten* (W. *mi mjed kyi 'jig rten*) in Tibetan, which means the world for the courageous ones, the world for the fearless ones. Among all the realms in the entire existence, this world, this human world where we are, is the most challenging world because beings, especially human beings, are very complicated and full of kleshas, the inner poisons such as greed, hatred, and delusion.

I know this sounds a little bit esoteric when we say we human beings are full of kleshas. You might think, "What do you mean, *klesha*?" It is a Sanskrit word, but if I really use very straight, down-to-earth, plain language, it means that we are neurotic. So we could call this the "loka of hang-ups," which is a very interesting term. "Loka" is a Sanskrit word for world, and you know the term "hang-up." This is the loka of hang-ups and therefore only the courageous ones have the guts to manifest in this world and deal with the suffering and craziness of everybody. This human world is in many ways a really wonderful world, but on the other hand it is extremely challenging.

Sometimes movies have wisdom that we are not expecting. This whole topic reminds me of the science fiction

41

movie *The Fifth Element*, in which negative forces are going to destroy the human world. An alien woman had the power to save the world, and a human hero charmed her heart, convincing her to do that. They had to get to a certain place to do a ceremony, and they were riding in a flying taxi. The alien woman got bored on the way, turned on the TV, and started channel surfing. She came across the history channel, which was showing the second World War. She was so turned off by the cruelty of the human race that she basically said she was not going to save this world. The hero had to work hard to change her mind, and they made it just in time to do the ceremony and save the human race.

Yet with all the trauma and tragedies that we go through, life is also unbelievably precious. There must be some reason why the courageous ones want to come here, even after they heard all the bad advertising about this world. You know, the universe already made an announcement: "There are so many different lokas. If you go to that loka, everybody is a saint. There, all you need to do is just hang around, and they will feed you. People are going to be kind and nice to you. Then if you go to that loka over there, everyone is a Buddha or bodhisattva. Nobody has the slightest impulse to hurt even a bird or insect. It is all benevolent. Then that world, the human world, is very challenging."

Of course, I am describing these things in a humorous fashion. You don't have to take the whole thing literally. By the way, when you read the teachings in this book, you don't have to take anything literally. Please understand that. You have to interpret them in a way that works for you. Some of these things you can take literally, other things you can take metaphorically. This is your teaching; it is not my teaching.

Anyway, these courageous ones must have some great reasons why they want to manifest here after hearing that life on earth is full of challenges. As we all know, if we walk the spiritual path, even trauma and tragedy become a blessing. Isn't this amazing? They become a gift because if we take these precious teachings to heart, we can embrace all our pain, suffering, trauma, and tragedy as an opportunity to manifest as a bodhisattva or even a Buddha.

Shantideva, the eighth-century author of *The Way of the Bodhisattva,* wrote that we should even be grateful for enemies:

> Since my adversary assists me in my bodhisattva
> way of life,
> I should long for him like a treasure discovered
> in the house
> and acquired without effort.

To be human is really to be a bodhisattva. This is our task, this is our vocation in this world, in this incarnation. The path of the bodhisattva is about not running away from life—from the messiness, the pain, and the wrath of this existence. It is about not being defeated, angry, or bitter, but learning to thrive and become more compassionate, more courageous. The bodhisattva's path is not to be afraid of living life fully but to continuously open our heart to the "ten-thousand joys and the ten-thousand sorrows."

Human beings are natural-born bodhisattvas if we really remember who we are and our duty in this incarnation. Therefore, we can use all our challenges and sorrows as a courageous path on which we can develop forgiveness, altruism, courage, compassion, and unconditional love. And in the end, we can even transcend the self. It is really possible.

There is a group of meditators who invited me to teach in the city of Baton Rouge, Louisiana. I went there many times to lead retreats for this small group because the friendship between us has been precious to me. There was one woman who came to the weekend meditation retreats a few times. She would often have a private meeting with me where she would share her difficulties. She had some kind of debilitating disease that could not be treated, which limited some of her functions. One time during our meeting, her language was very different. She didn't talk about all the turmoil that she was going through. She had a little sparkle and said, "I'm thankful for my disease. If it were not for that, I would not be who I am today." There was an obvious change that happened to her through her spiritual practice.

When I look at my own life, I can't really find many reports, such as reports on my spiritual awakening and so forth, to share with you. But I found that some shifts happened in my consciousness here and there. This is neither special nor unique because we all go through changes, if not by spirituality then simply by the merit of aging. I noticed that some of the shifts occurring in my consciousness are not so much because I have been practicing all the *sadhanas* and meditation. Instead, a little bit here and a little bit there, I have been trying to use the Buddhist teachings when I go through challenges. Now and then, when I'm lucky, I have some willingness to use the Buddhist teachings to embrace life's challenges as an opportunity to practice the Dharma— the Dharma of love, compassion, acceptance, and *bodhicitta*, the awakened heart.

The human heart is unbelievably resilient. It is a transcender in itself because if you allow yourself to be in touch with the best of yourself, regardless of what you went through or what you might be facing, you can always say, "All is well," and feel truly joyous inside.

WISDOM OF IMPERMANENCE

We can go on forever talking about the bardo of life, but let me go to the heart of the matter. Karma Lingpa wrote beautiful verses on the six bardos. In the first verse, he said, "Now that for once I have attained a human body, this is not the time to remain in the ways of distraction."

He is saying that this life is so short. He also said this is the only time that you have been born as a human. What he is saying is not to be taken literally. He is inviting us to meditate on the idea that this is the only time we are a human. Then with that recognition of how precious this incarnation is, there is an urgency not to waste this life and to make the best out of it. This is a powerful reflection. With such insight, we pay attention to things that are essential and experience the aspiration to wake up or help people or spend more time actively interested in a life of reflection. Karma Lingpa basically said, "Do not waste this precious life by being controlled by all the distractions."

This life is unbelievably short and transient, which makes it very precious. When you think about how old you are, some of you may realize that you are already halfway through this human incarnation. You may have the interesting feeling that the life you led for the last forty years is like a dream. It is all gone. When somebody asks you what you have been doing, you might say, "Well, I've been eating ..." We can't even say what we have been doing. There are very few memories left of that. The whole thing was like a dream, as if it never happened. Sometimes we have to look at our journals to remind ourselves of what we were doing even three or four years ago. Our conscious mind cannot actually remember our whole life—it is as if it all happened in a single moment of a dream.

And someday we will be dying. I hope we will know that we are dying when that time comes. Then when we look back, we will realize that this whole life on earth was just like a big dream. It is already dissolving. Therefore, the most important contemplation that we can carry in our everyday life is to realize that this human life is extremely transient, and we can die at any given moment.

Intellectually we know or understand the shortness of this precious, amazing human existence, our own life. But there is a different kind of quality when you really begin to feel the shortness of your own life in your bones, in your heart. This reflection has the potency to move you, to invoke something inside you, whereas the intellectual understanding of the shortness of life doesn't really have the potency to do that. This reflection invokes something unique and individual in each of us, but often it invokes an inner fire, the fire of longing, the desire to wake up... to wake up before it is too late, since this existence is quite short.

But perhaps our doctor told us a few days ago, "You're healthy. You don't really need to do anything. Maybe take more vitamin D, drink more water. Otherwise you're very healthy. Just do some exercise." Perhaps some of us have this very strong certainty that we are going to live for a very long time. It may be true that you might live until you are eighty years old, ninety years old, or maybe even beyond that. But even so, this human life is unbelievably short. There are giant trees that live longer than us. The giant redwood trees in Mendocino County in Northern California are perhaps the most amazing trees in the world. The redwood trees are beautiful; they are the tallest of all trees. But upon visiting and seeing these old trees that lived a thousand years ago, we realize how new we are to this earth and how short our time here is. I have this sense when I go to the redwood forest. There are even species of little fish, like rock fish, that live longer than us—they can live for one or two hundred years.

Some of us are middle-aged now. I remember many years ago, people said to me, "When you turn forty, you will do this and that; when you turn fifty then you will do this and that." I thought, "That is like the really far-distant future. They are talking now about what I'm going to do in the next few eons." But it is already happening, as you and I are experiencing, and it didn't take a really long time. This is how old age and the end of life are going to happen to us—as a shocking surprise.

A while ago, I was informed that a dear friend of mine had only six months to live. At that time, somebody asked me to talk about the most important subject in the Buddhist tradition: the truth of impermanence, that nothing is absolutely permanent. While many things are obviously transient, now and then we might have some beautiful delusion that there are things in this universe that are permanent because they are grand, eternal, sublime, or mighty. In the reflection on the truth of impermanence, we wake up and realize that not even one single thing in this existence is permanent. Not only that, we begin to see that everything is constantly changing. Such changes are so subtle that our ordinary mind cannot recognize them; they require a whole new level of attention and awareness.

Of course, we all know that change is not always bad, but sometimes it can be extremely painful. Impermanence can be extremely painful. You are probably able to come up with a whole list of things that you really love and appreciate in your life. For example, friendship is extremely precious. Perhaps one of the most precious gifts that we can have in this life is human friendship based on mutual trust, reverence, and the feeling that you and your friends are walking together on an amazing journey. Even friendship is impermanent because it can be lost to death or illness. We cannot hold onto anything, no matter how much we love it. Eventually, a lot of things that we love in this world are going to dissolve, even things in the realm of the natural world: species, trees, forests, as well as the greatest cities.

I have been working on some drawings, which are called Dharma cartoons. One of the Dharma cartoons is about a Buddhist wedding ceremony. Have you ever been to a Buddhist wedding ceremony? They are perhaps not as fancy as other wedding ceremonies. This cartoon is about a wedding ceremony where the ceremonial master was a Buddhist nun or monk. Two people are getting married and the Buddhist monk or nun says, "Now let's meditate on impermanence." One of the main features of a Buddhist wedding ceremony is to invite the newlywed couple and all their relatives to meditate on the most important message of Buddha, impermanence. Imagine that you are getting married right now, feeling that you found your soulmate, then somebody says, "This whole thing is impermanent." That may not be a very welcome message for you.

A lot of things in our lives make us happy, and we're not ready to simply say they are impermanent or illusory. But they are like a dream, a mirage. During the monsoon retreats in some monasteries, the monks or nuns used to chant a verse from the *Diamond Sutra* while making a circumambulation around the temple. The verse says, "One must regard all compounded things like a star, hallucination, butter lamp, bubble, magical illusion, dew, lightning, dream, and cloud." This verse sounds a little bit pessimistic in some sense because it is inviting all of us to see the whole world as an illusion, like a dream. But it turns out the verse has a very inspiring and uplifting message. It is not about being sad or depressed, thinking that nothing has meaning. It is inviting us to be lighthearted by not taking things as too real, not taking things too seriously. That is the message of this verse. In the ultimate sense, to be lighthearted is our ability to see that pretty much everything that we are holding onto in this life is impermanent, like a dream, an illusion.

Impermanence is a very liberating truth. It is like an existential gift given by the universe. Imagine if we were going to live here forever or that conditions would never change. That would be quite bad; it could even be a curse. One of the mantras that you can recite is a famous phrase that comes from a fable: "This too shall pass." Perhaps many of you have heard this fable about a powerful king who gathered all of the wise men and commanded them to come up with wisdom words that would be accurate all the time. The group of wise men went back, reflected, and had a discussion among themselves. The phrase they finally came up with was "This too shall pass." They said this wisdom was always going to be accurate in all circumstances. They even inscribed the phrase on a ring and presented it to the king. And the king was pleased.

I sometimes encourage people to contemplate this phrase, this wisdom, in order to realize that when we go through suffering and pain, when we are struggling with very painful situations, they are not permanent. Soon or later they all will go away. Now and then when people talk to me, they share their tragedy and their struggles. And sometimes I will tell them, "Just stay as courageous as possible, and someday this whole thing will be just a memory." Similarly, everything will be a memory someday. At the time when we are dying, this whole life will be memory. Even this life that we are holding onto will pass. The life that you are loving, the life that you're struggling with, is going to pass eventually.

The wisdom of impermanence has many profound aspects. One is the realization that we always have to face impermanence and not get too attached to anything. Through the reflection on impermanence, there will be wisdom in our consciousness that reminds us that we always have to be ready to let go and to embrace death, loss, and change.

Perhaps you may have heard the Buddhist joke about a man who was walking but wasn't very mindful. He fell off a cliff, but he was able to hold onto a branch of a tree. He knew sooner or later that he was going to fall down, so he started shouting and praying to the Buddha. He said, "Buddha, help me."

After praying for a long time, suddenly a calm and noble voice arose from the sky and said, "Let go."

After a pause, the man said, "Is there anyone else out there?"

The bardo teachings help us to maintain the wisdom of impermanence and be ready to let go, so when some change happens in our life, perhaps we won't be angry. We will be able to ground ourselves in love, compassion, and acceptance. This is the benefit of practicing the reflection on impermanence and studying these teachings on the bardo.

Have you ever had a near-death experience? I never had a near-death experience—that can be a very mystical experience —but I had an event in which I thought I might die. It was caused by a really strong pain in the left side of my body that happened around five years ago due to some injury. Some of my friends were with me at that time and were an extremely strong source of love and friendship. I had to go into the hospital, as I was in excruciating pain. I never had such strong pain like that, and my mind started going a little bit crazy. I started entertaining the thought that I might die because I didn't know what was happening; the pain was very intense. No conditions had ever brought me that very vivid sense of the awareness of my own mortality.

When I thought I might possibly die, I prayed, "Please, universe, give me a chance to live more. Please let me live more." Not because I wanted to have more ice cream or something like that. Part of me said, "I haven't finished my work in this life. There are people who are dependent on me, people who need me." I had the realization that I had taken for granted so many precious moments when I could have been doing something meaningful for people. It was a very interesting experience to be between the pain, the painful awareness of my possible mortality, and the desire to live. It is not that I had all kinds of desires like, "Oh, I want to live because then I can drive my sporty car. I am not ready to die, because I just bought my Ferrari." I didn't have a fancy sporty car. It wasn't anything like that. It was that I wanted to live so I could continue some of my work that I felt wasn't finished and to help those who were very dependent on me. There wasn't so much self-interest.

During this time when my own impermanence became quite pronounced, I had an image in my mind that we are all cosmic travelers riding a train. You might call it the train of eternity, which continues to travel. It's like the train that people ride from one end of the continent to the other, with many interesting stops along the way. I felt that we are all cosmic travelers and this life is just another train station where we all get out and talk to each other, or buy some local goods if there are shops. And we can run into trouble periodically, maybe with another cosmic traveler, or maybe somebody is trying to sell us some local goods, and we end up arguing about the price. We think that we have been here forever when actually we have been riding that train of eternity and soon we have to get back on the train.

Our human life is constantly dancing between two dynamic energies, which Buddhism calls *du drel* (W. *'du 'brel*), meeting and separation. This turns out to be particularly true in human relationships. People somehow come into our life, and eventually we all separate, sometimes too soon, sometimes just by a natural process, such as losing your friend to illness, death, or other inevitable situations.

With the awareness of death, we begin to receive meaningful reminders from life. One reminder was spoken by Padampa Sangye, a twelfth-century Indian master who came to ancient Tibet. He was one of the most celebrated Buddhist Mahasiddhas and the master and guru to Machig Labdron, a very famous female Tibetan Mahasiddha. He gave a synthesized version of his teachings to the people of Tingri in Western Tibet, known as *One Hundred Verses of Advice*. This text encapsulates not only the essential wisdom of Padampa but also the essential wisdom of the entire Buddhist teachings. One very poignant verse says,

> Families are as fleeting as a crowd on market day;
> People of Tingri, don't bicker or fight.

Our life is just like the gathering of the market. When the market opens, people come from everywhere. They trade with each other. Perhaps they eat and converse with each other. Then evening falls, everybody leaves the market, and it remains empty. It is a very powerful image. Sooner or later, everyone is going to depart from this world. Padampa said, "Do not fight. Do not squabble." This is a very important verse, which we often quote in the Buddhist teachings. It means that the people you love, such as your family members, the whole family structure, is impermanent, and sooner or later your family members will go away. Life calls them to take a whole new path, or perhaps they all die one after another. This is such a powerful reminder for everybody—for families, for communities, for a nation, for a tribe, and for all of humanity as well.

What I'm trying to say is we have to live with the contemplation that this life is extremely short, and it can dissolve at any given moment. Therefore, we need to bring about a strong aspiration, the intention to wake up.

It is said that monks and nuns in Tibet used to write two phrases on their walls: *chi wa* (W. *'chi ba*), death, and *ma yeng* (W. *ma yengs*), do not be distracted. Every time they looked around, there were these reminders rather than pictures of their grandmother, expensive plates, or the TV. Simply looking at the phrases, you remember that death can happen at any moment. It inspires you to do whatever matters most to yourself. "Do not be distracted" means not to get lost in frivolous activities or frivolous states of mind but rather to be present and focus on what matters.

THREE PRACTICES

Karma Lingpa's verse on the bardo of life goes on to say, "Enter, undistracted, the path of study, reflection and meditation." In Karma Lingpa's words, the assignment for the first bardo is to engage with these three observances, which are found in many traditions in the East. They are used as the framework for spiritual practice.

Studying is a part of all the great traditions as well as part of human civilization. Everything we know, not just about the sacred but even about ordinary things, comes from studying. It is not that suddenly we figure out everything. Of course, now and then, we do have our own innovations, but many things we do in everyday life have knowledge behind them, and a huge part of knowledge is acquired from studying.

Study was so important that in the old days, many monks and nuns spent a great deal of time learning the Buddhist scriptures. Great learning centers were created, such as Nalanda, the great university in ancient India. In Tibet, many monasteries often have two schools known as *shedra (W. bshad grwa)* and *drupdra (W. sgrub grwa)*. Shedra is the school of study where monks and nuns emphasize studying the scriptures, while drupdra is the school where they emphasize meditation practice.

Study is not about becoming erudite and acquiring huge amounts of philosophical knowledge. Instead, study is a form of spiritual practice that can inspire us and give us insight into the path of love, wisdom, and the nature of reality. Study is an important factor for our inner freedom because through it, we engage with the inner work that will undo our delusion and neuroses.

In the Buddhist tradition, sometimes you may study one classical text for a while. But study does not always involve working on some text or scripture. Study also includes studying with somebody, therefore the term for study in Sanskrit is *shrūta*, or in Tibetan, *tuh pa* (W: *thos pa*), both of which mean "to hear" or "to listen," such as listening to someone giving a teaching or a commentary. Often, when you listen to somebody whose teachings resonate with you, your whole being is affected in that moment, and your mind and heart are changed. Looking into the history of your inner spiritual development, you may find that reading a book or hearing a teaching inspired you to do some inner work that eventually resulted in inner growth or transformation. Personally, I am often moved and inspired when I listen to someone give beautiful teachings coming from his or her own heart. I think this is a common experience for many people. There is a spiritual transmission happening all the time. It is like a lineage that continues in every culture throughout history. All the values we have learned in our life were not just invented in the last decade. They have been taught and passed from one generation to the next.

In the monasteries, sometimes you have a chance to listen to the Buddhist teachings every day. It's just part of your life.

But in the modern secular world, many people don't really have the opportunity to listen to spiritual teachings because the world is lacking a sacred infrastructure. A society with sacred infrastructure might encourage us to get up early in the morning and study a sacred scripture each day. But our modern society is more about surviving, working hard, and being entertained. We get up, check our messages, go to work, eat, watch our TV series, and go to bed. Then we have a vacation, we plan to go to France or Bali…we don't say that in our next free time we will go on a pilgrimage. Everything in the news is about what is happening in the world. Driving in the car, we see all the billboards; on the radio, we hear all the talk shows. There is not a sense of a sacred infrastructure where you have the good fortune to hear spiritual teachings. It requires a lot of your own effort and many circumstances coming together to even listen to spiritual teachings. I think this is true for many people in the world. Also, sometimes when you hear spiritual teachings, you may find they are filled with dualism, concepts, or dogma. It is very hard to hear spiritual teachings that point out love and true awakening.

Karma Lingpa is encouraging us to listen to spiritual teachings as much as possible in everyday life. Study invites us to pay attention to the sacred, to enlightenment, to nirvana, to awareness, to love, as well as to the path. Studying the sacred teachings will inspire us to develop the aspiration or intention to wake up and to understand the means for enlightenment.

Reflection, in Tibetan, *sampa* (W. *bsam pa*), in Sanskrit *chinta*, can be related to the first practice, study or listening. For example, in the Buddhist tradition, you might be studying special themes like bodhicitta, no-self, or awakened heart. Then you go back and review those teachings to make sure that you understand them. That is one form of reflection. This is very good because sometimes while listening to spiritual teachings misunderstandings can arise.

Reflection also happens naturally in certain settings. For example, during a retreat, you may spend some time reflecting on spiritual matters in our life, such as love, compassion, and existential questions. In ordinary life, the reflection may be very mundane...about politics, weather, our financial situation, education, and so forth. Our reflection may not be a sacred or existential reflection that can challenge our perception or value system. Most of our daily reflections don't have a sacred component that helps us evolve. Sacred reflection is not usually in our life unless we make a special effort to engage in it.

The third observance is meditation, *bhavana* in Sanskrit, *gom* (W. *sgom)* in Tibetan, both of which mean "to become familiar." Meditation is perhaps the most amazing inner work human beings can do. But it is very vast. It cannot be defined as one dimensional. The etymology of *gom*, or *bhavana,* has the connotation of repeating something in your mind again and again so that you become familiar with it. For example, if you meditate on love again and again, eventually your whole being becomes familiar with love.

Traditionally, all meditations can be categorized into *shamata* and *vipashyana*. Shamata is the meditation practice that quiets our mind. The second one, vipashyana, is the practice that helps us see the falsehood of our beliefs and illusions. Our life is run by so many illusions, including the collective and personal narratives that we wholeheartedly buy into. Meditation helps us to see the true nature of reality, or the way things are. It is quite important for people to have a daily meditation practice. They may choose a specific time of the day, where they can meditate, either one or a few times a day. The chapter on the bardo of meditation will go into this in more detail.

The study of the bardos can go on for a while. Please regard the teachings as something you will take into your life and start working with every day if you can. In Tantric Buddhism, there are essential or synthesized liturgies that people recite as their daily spiritual practice, called *gyün khyer* (W. *rgyun khyer*), daily practice. This model can be applied to our own spiritual practice. You can do some formal spiritual practices such as chanting liturgies or sitting meditation.

It is also nice to begin the day by setting a sacred intention when you wake up. The morning is the most important time of day, like the window of opportunity to decide what kind of day you want to live. Therefore, you could chant any kind of sacred liturgy, beautiful poems, or you can compose your own sacred aphorisms. A friend of mine once told me that he composed his own aphorism that he repeated each day: "May I be free from self-concern." This is such a powerful way to transform oneself. One time I also composed my own sacred aphorisms. They are very useful when I don't have time to chant a long, thick liturgy. They also give me the essentials. I use words like: "May I live as a bodhisattva. May I not react to what arises from my old habits. May I be able to meet the world with courage and compassion. May I remain in awareness."

It is very challenging for most people to go through authentic inner transformation unless they have some kind of daily spiritual practice. If we are not mindful, we unconsciously repeat all our old mental habits constantly. Therefore, the Tibetan masters made a commitment to themselves—and encouraged us—to always be mindful and never fall prey to unconscious habits, even for a single moment. Eleventh-century master Langri Thangpa said:

> In my every action, I will watch my mind,
> And the moment destructive emotions arise,
> I will confront them strongly and avert them,
> Since they will hurt both me and others.

Recognize that what wastes this lifetime is being lost in frivolous states of mind. Make a personal vow and hold an intention not to get distracted in these mental states. Vow to be fully present, loving what is unfolding.

PART II:
BARDO OF DREAMING

ཀྱེ་མ༔ བདག་ལ་རྨི་ལམ་བར་དོ་འཆར་དུས་འདིར༔

གཏི་མུག་རོ་ཉལ་བག་མེད་སྤངས་བྱས་ནས༔

དྲན་པ་ཡེངས་མེད་གནས་ལུགས་ངང་ལ་འཇོག༔

རྨི་ལམ་བ་ཟུང་ནས་སྤྲུལ་བསྒྱུར་འོད་གསལ་སྤྱང༔

དུད་འགྲོ་བཞིན་དུ་ཉལ་བར་མ་བྱེད་ཅིག༔

གཉིད་དང་མཐོན་སུམ་འདྲེས་པའི་ཉམས་ལེན་གཅེས༔

Kyema! Now when the bardo of dream appears,
I will abandon unconscientiousness
and the corpse-like sleep of ignorance,
And abide undistractedly in the natural state of the mind.
Recognizing dreams, I will train in transformation
and clear light;
I must not simply slumber like an animal.
It is essential to integrate sleep with direct realization.

Bardo of Dreaming

The second bardo is the bardo of dreaming, in Tibetan, *milam bardo* (W. *rmi lam bar do*). Dreams are mentioned quite extensively in the Buddhist teachings. In the sutras, Buddha often used dreams as one of the most powerful metaphors to describe the nature of our illusory life or illusory existence. Therefore, there is a lot of contemplation on dreams in Buddhist practice. Many people in the Western world are interested in dream analysis and dream interpretation. Even though dream analysis is mentioned in various ancient Buddhist texts, it is not the main focus of the practices of the dream bardo such as dream yoga.

At the same time, it can be useful to analyze your dreams from time to time. There is a saying in Tibetan Buddhism that your realization, your spiritual progress, is measured and determined by your conduct and your dreams, which is quite an interesting idea. It is said, "The degree of your inner awakening is measured by your dreams. Signs of your inner awakening are revealed through your actions." This is very applicable to Tantric Buddhist practice. The idea is that you can analyze your dreams to get a picture of where you are in your spiritual growth and how much progress you are making. And obviously your actions are a clear barometer of your inner spiritual growth. If you are truly compassionate, often the world will witness that through your actions and what you do with people.

If anybody is truly interested in personal evolution, one step that cannot be easily maneuvered around is the acquisition of self-knowledge. Dreams can be a very wonderful medium through which we can understand ourselves, through which self-knowledge can be cultivated. We are able to look back at our dreams and recognize some of our predominating neuroses. We can see feelings that we suppressed, trauma that didn't heal, or see our shadows that came up in the dream. Dreams can be useful for those of us interested in spiritual awakening because we can analyze the dream and see what is happening in our life as well as in the dark recesses of our psyche. They show us our bright side and how evolved we are—our aspiration and goodness—as well as our unfinished baggage, our shadow, and all our neurotic stuff.

When I was young, I had incredible devotion and love for Guru Padmasambhava. It is very hard to describe this devotion to modern people, but sacred devotion is an important part of many cultures. When you go to Mexico, there are so many images of Our Lady of Guadalupe. When you see these statues, you can feel that the people in that culture have so much devotion toward her. The same is true in India, which is a culture that has been rooted in devotion for millennia. Devotion is not some kind of strange phenomenon. In some cultures, it is all pervasive.

I had very strong devotion to Padmasambhava because I was raised by grandparents who loved Padmasambhava. One of the first sacred images I saw in my life was the *thangka*, a sacred painting, of Padmasambhava that my grandparents had on their altar. They used to recite the names of Padmasambhava, and they prayed to him. When I was young, I had such strong love for Padmasambhava and his teachings that every night before I fell asleep I usually recited a long prayer to him called *söl dep leu dün ma* (W. *gsol 'debs le'u bdun ma*), which has seven chapters. I did this many nights for more than one year.

Then at some point, I had a lot of wonderful dreams. I dreamt that I was flying in the sky and visiting Padmasambhava in all the beautiful realms. I felt ecstatic, like I was receiving extraordinary teachings. I went to his paradise where he was smiling at me and granting his blessings. That kind of dream kept occurring in my life for a few years. Eventually those kinds of dreams stopped, and my dreams got a little bit mundane. My dream state descended totally. It should be the other way around but in my case, they started descending. Nowadays, my dreams are not bad; they are neither good nor bad. I don't have all those holy dreams, except now and then. But I don't really have very ordinary dreams that bother me either. At least I am comfortable with my dream world.

Much later in my life I had some dreams that I used as a means for understanding my state of consciousness as well as my old habits, which can be so subtle. One time, I had a dream where I was at a huge gathering with a lot of other people. One person was sitting on the stage with unmarked boxes. This gentleman, who had a loudspeaker, was doing a ceremony called animal release where people free animals who are going to be killed, thus saving their lives. In my dream, I had a strong identity of myself as a Buddhist who should do something wholesome. Then each person picked up a box, which was supposed to contain an animal. But no one knew which animal they would get. I picked up one box, opened it, and saw it was full of cockroaches. Immediately I felt aversion and wanted to throw it away and get another box. But I noticed everyone was watching me, and I would be judged as not being compassionate. So with a happy expression, I pretended to like that box, even though I really didn't want it.

Later when I woke up, I thought it was a very strange dream. Usually dreams relate to something in your life, but this one had no context related to my daily life. I revisited that dream for a long time as a way to understand what was happening in my consciousness. It told me that obviously I had a judgment about cockroaches because they became an object for my own aversion. It has nothing to do with the cockroaches. They are just doing their own thing. They are made out of molecules just like everything else. But I had aversion to them because we all are a little brainwashed by the collective consensus. Cockroaches are treated as repulsive even though there is not one single reason it is true. They are not repulsive in themselves, any more than any other species. But we are taught they are repulsive, then we develop our own perception based on that. I began to see the very subtle judgment that I had to transcend. I also discovered I had an egoic motive that cared about other people's opinions. In my dream, I was really attached to how I looked to others and realized this was something I should cut through.

So you can use dreams as a mirror of self-reflection to find out what sort of karmic habits you are still dealing with. Maybe there are some strong karmic habits or kleshas that you haven't noticed, but they are there, and they often tend to appear in the dream state. Then you can take that understanding, that self-knowledge, into your spiritual practice to work on what is unpurified, or to work on the gross as well as subtle kleshas that are deeply rooted in your psyche but are not normally known to you.

At the same time, we should not get into dream analysis too much. It is not like we have to analyze every dream we have. We don't have to interpret them either. In my dream, there was nothing to interpret—the cockroaches were cockroaches, and the aversion was aversion. It's not necessary to write all our dreams down. That can be too much. Many times, our dreams are just mental chatter. There is not much logic in the dream. Perhaps you saw somebody a few days ago, and you also went to a coffee shop one day. Then you have a dream where you are meeting that person in the coffee shop. Your mind is putting all the disconnected data together.

One time Dakpopa, one of the main disciples of Milarepa, had an exquisite dream, which he shared with his master. Milarepa first said that in general, dreams are illusion. Just like that, many dreams are not worth taking too seriously. Then Milarepa told Dakpopa that while dreams are generally not worthy of being taken seriously, this dream was important. Milarepa then gave a whole commentary on the dream. He then said:

> ...you should know that this life is merely a part of the bardos of birth and death; its experiences are unreal and illusory, a form of reinforced dreaming. Mental activity in the daytime creates a latent form of habitual thought, which transforms itself at night into various delusory visions sensed by consciousness. This is called the deceptive and magic-like bardo of dream.

In the sleep state, all the sensory awareness functions of our consciousness are temporarily in hibernation in the state of consciousness known as *alaya*. The workings of the alaya act as the basis for all our habits and experiences, which continue in our dream and sleep. The alaya, or the storehouse-like foundation, is a psychic phenomenon or state of mind that functions as the train that carries all our habits from this moment to the next moment, from this day to the next day, from this month to the next month, until some kind of breakthrough takes place.

During the process of falling asleep, the so-called *mano-vijnana*, or mental consciousness, arises from the alaya. The mano-vijnana is one of the eight consciousnesses according to the ancient school of thought called *Chittamatra*, or mind-only school. The whole journey of falling asleep has a correlation with the dying process. It is said that by practicing dream yoga, one can prepare to have awareness during the dying process.

It is crucial to bring attention to the dream state because it is not a completely innocent state of consciousness. There is a belief even among spiritual practitioners that we don't have to attend to our consciousness in the dreaming state as long as we are attending to our consciousness during the day. But it is not as if we can say, "As long as I'm aware, awake, practicing meditation and awareness during the day, I don't really have to worry about what happens in my consciousness during my dreaming state. It's just a dream. I'm not responsible." Or one might say, "I just want to have nice sleep and not worry about anything." The dream state is not as innocent as we might think.

There is also an idea that there is not so much you can do when you go to sleep and dream; that the dream has its own independent life, so you don't have to take care of it. Therefore sometimes for meditators, the end of spiritual practice is when they are ready to fall asleep. Then they take a really long break—depending on how long they are going to sleep, it might be eight hours.

But Tantric Buddhism says otherwise. It tells us that when we are dreaming, we are pretty much the same person. We are in the same body, obviously. Not only that, the consciousness that continues through the dream state is almost the same consciousness that we are living in during the day. It is the same consciousness that carries all our habits—our not-so-wholesome habits as well as our wholesome habits. It is said that whatever we experience during the day tends to continue through the night in our consciousness unless some shift happens through intentional methods, such as the practice of awareness.

Tantric Buddhism teaches that our samsaric habits—the habits that bind us to the world of suffering—are often stored in the different dimensions of our being: in our consciousness, in our body, in our subtle body, as well as in our dreams, which are also a state of consciousness. Therefore, Tantric Buddhism invites us to pay attention to these old karmic patterns that are stored in our subtle body and in our mind. Those karmic habits can continue to perpetuate themselves in the dream state, and a very powerful process of karmic purification can happen through the dream.

There was a very famous Dzogchen master named Khenpo Ngakgi Wangpo in the Kham region of Tibet. It is said that one time a man showed up at the monastery where Khenpo Ngakgi was living at the time. The man said he had

71

been a hunter, had killed a lot of animals, and had been leading a low life. He was feeling regret, and he realized that he was getting old and was afraid of death. He offered bows to the lama and said, "Please purify all my karmas right now." The lama sat for a while, then said with a stern expression, "This is not something I can do. I cannot purify your karma." The old man was devastated and didn't want to leave. Then the lama said, "Since you are so sincere, why don't you sleep in the temple tonight? Just be sure to stay the whole night, until morning." This was an unusual suggestion, since the temple is holy and sacred, and Tibetans don't usually sleep in the temple at night.

So the old man went into the temple and slept as the lama told him. All night he had nightmares and was terribly tormented by his dreams. It was unbearable. Toward the end of the night, his dreams got a little bit better. He dreamt he was a wolf passing by the famous pile of mantra stones built by Patrul Rinpoche. Then the old man woke up and went back to the lama, who already knew what had happened without anyone saying anything. The lama was smiling and said, "Well, your karma is now purified. Lead a noble life from now on." His karma had been exhausted in the dream state.

It is important to realize that the dream state is a huge part of life. It not only carries what we experience during day-to-day life, but it can carry karmic data, an entire stream of memories, emotions, moods, and knowable as well as unknowable mental formations.

During the dream state, usually we lose awareness and don't realize we are dreaming. This is why people tend to suffer when they have nightmares, for example. You may know some people who suffer a lot through dreaming. I know a few people who tend to have recurring nightmares, or they tend to have quite frightening or not very wholesome dreams, and they suffer as a result. Of course, they don't make a big deal out of it. People don't say, "Well, I really have a lot of bad dreams. That's why I've come to see you." People don't usually go to see a spiritual teacher or psychotherapist because they have some unwholesome dreams. But there are people who are suffering from dreams that have a lot of fear, or if not fear, a lot of anger. I think if you had a dream with a lot of fear, you might go to see a therapist or spiritual teacher. But if it is a dream that has a lot of anger, hatred, judgment, or greed, you might not think that you have to do something with that kind of recurring dream.

The problem with the dream state is that we often lose awareness to such an extent that we believe that a dream is no longer a dream. We think it is complete reality just the way we believe what is happening right now is totally real. This delusion was pointed out by great masters of the past. For example, Taoist master Chuang Tzu said,

> Once upon a time, I dreamt I was a butterfly, fluttering hither and thither. I was conscious only of my happiness as a butterfly, unaware that I was Chuang Tzu. Soon I awakened, and there I was, myself again. Now I do not know whether I was a man dreaming I was a butterfly or whether I am now a butterfly, dreaming I am a man.

There is a classic story in Vedanta about a king called Janaka who lived in ancient India. One day the king was taking a nap on his bed with his servants fanning him and his soldiers standing guard outside the door. As he dozed off, he had a dream that the neighboring kingdom defeated him, and he was taken prisoner and was tortured. As he felt the torture begin, Janaka woke up from the dream with sweat on his face. He looked around, and he was lying in his bed with the servants still fanning him. He dozed off once again and had the same dream. He woke up and again was safe. He became disturbed: while he was asleep, the world of his dream seemed so real; awake, the world of the senses seems real. He asked all the sages, "Which is real, the waking state or the dream state?" No one could answer. Finally a young boy named Ashtavakra came and told him, "Your Majesty, neither your waking state nor the dreaming state is real." The king asked, "Then what is real?" The young sage replied, "The state beyond these two. Explore that. That alone is the reality."

Sometimes during the day, as a yogi or meditator, we may wake up and realize, "Oh, this is not real. This is my own projection," and we come back to awareness. This can happen quite often during the day for a meditator. But during a dream, even though you are wonderful meditators, unless you had some training on the dream bardo and dream yoga, you may not have any kind of discipline to cultivate awareness while you are dreaming in the same way you are cultivating awareness, vigilance, or mindfulness during the day. So sooner or later, you have to pay attention to dreams.

The Buddhist masters have been exploring the nature of dreams for centuries, resulting in profound insight about dreams and methods for working with them. Without having any kind of training or method to work with dreams, it is possible that we are perpetuating all our old habits and the three poisons in the dream state. This can have an impact on our overall consciousness. For example, if we have a lot of mundane dreams where we are involved in unwholesome states of mind like anger or fear, it affects us even in the waking state.

It might be helpful to review a dream that you had or are having these days. You might even like to go back to when you were little and try to remember the kind of dreams that you had then. Perhaps you remember that you had a lot of ordinary, fearful dreams or dreamt that you were fighting with people. Or you were competing with people, or somebody was trying to hurt you and you were very frightened. Or maybe you were worried about your achievements in a dream. Maybe you had a dream that you were taking an exam at school but you failed, and you became totally unhappy. Did you ever have those dreams? You can have all kinds of dreams that stir up all the ordinary inner poisons, which can leave a residue in your consciousness.

Sometimes if you are totally engaged with spiritual practices, the nature of your dreams can change. You will often have very positive or quite enlightened dreams where you are practicing generosity, you are meditating, you are happy, or you are quite joyous in a good way. Even in the ancient Buddhist scriptures, it is said that, for example, when you have a dream of meditating in the company of monks and nuns, it is a sign that you are on the path of awakening.

The nature of dreams is illusion. This is the most important thing to remember in the dream bardo: the nature of dreams is illusion. Dreams are not real. They are a mental phenomenon. Dreams have no concrete reality. It is all just happening in our consciousness no matter how powerful, how convincing, how joyous, or how fearful it may be. It is all happening as a complete mental phenomenon with not the slightest speck of reality.

DREAM YOGA

The traditional teachings on the bardo of dreaming are not so much about the nature of dreams but about the practices that we can use to bring awareness into the dream state. The practice of awareness in the dream state is called dream yoga. This practice has three points: recognition, transformation, and clear light. Padmasambhava said,

> Recognize the dream, then train in transformation
> and clear light.
> Do not slumber like an animal.
> The practice of integrating sleep with direct realization
> is crucial.

Recognizing Dreams

The first point is called recognizing dreams as dreams. This involves some techniques, although the techniques vary between traditions. Each master as well as each tradition within Tantric Buddhism developed slightly different techniques to help us develop the awareness or mental

Tantric
Buddhism =
VAJRAYANA

capacity to recognize a dream as a dream. Some of these methods are a little bit interesting and may seem complex if you are not familiar with Vajrayana or Tantric Buddhism. Therefore, let me share the simplest method with you.

The first step in recognizing dreams as dreams is to set an intention. As you prepare for sleep, you say, "May I have the ability to recognize dreams as dreams." You say that at least once, either out loud or in silence. The direct translation of the traditional prayer is, "May you grant blessings upon me so I may recognize dreams as dreams." But you can use your own translation or just say, "May I have the ability to recognize dreams as dreams." You say that once, and then usually your intention would be established. The bardo teachings say to make sure that this thought is established before you fall asleep. There is some kind of impact of the last thought you have before you totally fall asleep. So the idea here is to make this intention the last thought you have when you go into the state of sleep. If you feel that the intention is not well established in your mind, then you say it again and again. "May I be able to recognize dreams as dreams."

The traditional dream yoga lays out very specific instructions including how to lie down, which direction to point your head, which side of your body to sleep on, and so forth. Many details are involved in it but here, the quintessence is to have an intention and to go to bed as if you are conducting a ceremony. Usually ceremonies are conducted not with a sloppy manner but with solemnity and carefulness. You might like to make sure your bed is comfortable. Then instead of just rushing into bed as usual, you might sit for a bit in a meditative posture before you lie down. Even when you lie down, you make sure your body is relaxed. Padmasambhava said, "Do not slumber like an animal."

Animals don't have rituals, and they go unconscious even though they might be uncomfortable. They sleep wherever they find a place…in the living room, on your bed, under the table. It fits them perfectly, but as humans, we want to add more awareness.

Visualization

Then the practice continues with a visualization. Visualization is very personal and depends on your background. Some instructions teach you to visualize different syllables in different parts of the body. A very simple method is to visualize a syllable or sacred image in your throat or heart.

In the Nyingma tradition, we visualize Guru Padmasambhava in the throat or heart. This is a very powerful method for those who have been practicing in the Nyingma lineage because we have developed so much affinity toward Guru Padmasambhava. There are different ways of understanding the principle of Guru Padmasambhava.

For many meditators in the Nyingma tradition, Guru Padmasambhava represents more than the historical Padmasambhava, the Mahasiddha who brought Tantric Buddhism and Dzogchen to Tibet in the eighth century. Guru Padmasambhava is considered an expression of the Dharmakaya, our true nature. Many religious traditions have their own version of the holy trinity. In Mahayana Buddhism, the trinity is Dharmakaya, Sambhogakaya, and Nirmanakaya. They are considered different dimensions of enlightenment, but the Dharmakaya is considered the highest, the source of all of them. The way of interpreting Dharmakaya is not always the same from one tradition to another. In nondual teachings such as Dzogchen, Dharmakaya represents the nature of our mind that is emptiness. It is not a being, a person, or an entity. It is totally formless. And yet it is in each of us. It is the true nature of our consciousness. Therefore, it is the most secret, the holiest, the most profound, the ineffable, and Guru Padmasambhava is an expression of that. Guru Padmasambhava represents nondual awareness, awakening to the absolute truth, the awareness of emptiness, no-self, bodhicitta, and so forth.

Because of the power of their training, sometimes when they visualize Guru Padmasambhava, many Nyingmapa yogis and yoginis can literally go into nondual awareness, a state of consciousness that is not centered in the ego. Isn't this amazing? All they need to do is visualize Guru Padmasambhava. Suddenly nondual awareness—the remembrance of their true nature as a non-egoic being, the unborn Buddha, the primordial Buddha—that awareness just pops up, if I can say that. The visualization is all they need.

Guru Padmasambhava as a representation of nondual awareness is an illustration of how we can use symbols as a method or a teaching. Symbols and images also invoke certain experiences, such as devotion, joy, love, and compassion. Many traditions say that you can use words and language to describe something totally profound only to a certain extent. Eventually you have to go beyond words to truly understand that which is profound, that which is ineffable. In contemporary society, we have a dilemma—we use language and words, and we try to understand everything through them. Then when we don't understand something, we reject it. This is why we have so many problems between doctrines or traditions. We are using imperfect means to understand that which goes beyond language: the ineffable.

Visualizations and symbols are all related to your training and your spiritual background. We are not saying that the only way that you can do the dream bardo practice is by visualizing Padmasambhava. In dream yoga, some of you might want to visualize Buddha, Kuan Yin, Tara, or even some extraordinary human Mahasiddhas like Yeshe Tsogyal or Machig Labdron. You can also visualize deities or the Divine from other traditions too. Therefore, when you lie down, you can visualize Guru Padmasambhava or any sacred image that you have a deep connection with. Don't worry about what you're doing. Just use it as a technique.

ༀ *Ah*

If you don't really know how to visualize deities, Mahasiddhas, Buddhas, or bodhisattvas, or don't feel comfortable visualizing them, you can visualize a syllable or a letter. One of the letters that is often recommended is the Tibetan letter *Ah (see the image above)*. *Ah* is more than a letter. The sound of *Ah* as well as the image of *Ah* are both symbols in the Eastern tradition. When somebody utters *Ah*, it is more than just uttering *Ah*. The sound of *Ah* represents the ultimate truth, the ineffable, the great emptiness, bodhicitta. I have to use all these words, even though they sound very abstract—emptiness, bodhicitta, nondual awareness. I have no choice except to use these words. These words can sound so flowery, but they are not flowery; they are as real as anything else. You all know that. You may have had many moments of witnessing these transcendent notions.

For example, in a meditation retreat, these terms become quite real for us, but then we can forget what we experienced. People can also have a very strong resistance to anything that has to do with transcendence or absolute truth, the idea that there is no self or that we are the indescribable Buddha, primordial awareness. But when we go to a meditation retreat, or when we go into silence or do some powerful silent sitting —in whatever form: Zen, Dzogchen, Vajrayana, or our own thing—sometimes something breaks in our consciousness. Then everything is primordial awareness, nonduality, emptiness, Buddha mind, Dharmakaya. The experience becomes so real, to the extent that everything else—self, birth, death, worry, anger, resentment, me, you—becomes a little unreal. The whole earthly reality becomes illusory. Perhaps you've had this experience many times.

Then we come back to the mundane world and forget what we experienced. Not only that, we even develop resistance to what we experienced, to what we can experience when our heart is open. The truth is that until we truly open our heart and mind and wake up to the ineffable, we won't be completely free, completely liberated. We will be stuck in the trap of ego and the trap of duality. But it is so difficult to describe the ineffable in words and concepts. It just doesn't work. Maybe this is why one time, Mahasiddha Saraha's wife and guru, who was called Arrow Maker, told him, "You can only understand Buddha's secret through symbols."

So image of *Ah,* as well as its sound, is a symbol. *Ah* represents pure awareness, great emptiness, all-pervasive sacredness, or suchness, whatever you like to call it. Or your true nature, your Buddhanature, the dimension of you that is already enlightened, that is totally untouched by ego. Remember, that which is most profound can often be overlooked. *Ah* can represent it or at least you can train your mind to associate the *Ah* syllable with awareness or with a representation of the highest sacredness if all these notions—emptiness, unborn, deathless, the unconditioned, the big mind, the Dharmakaya—don't fit your paradigm.

As you are concentrating on the image of the *Ah* syllable in your throat, you might like to visualize it radiating with a bright color. Then that visualization of *Ah* also blocks all your thoughts, which is amazing. Often when you go to bed, you may have a lot of thoughts, a busy mind. Maybe you open your smartphone before falling asleep, you get lost in the news cycle, and you see some bad things happening here, some bad things happening over there. Or maybe you revisit or review the day and feel very strong emotions. Perhaps there is a physical impact from some unpleasant meeting that you had. Maybe you are worried about what happened during the day. Maybe you are worried about your life, or you are worried about the future, or maybe you are really worried about what clothes you are going to wear tomorrow. Our mind is sometimes very active. Not only that, it can get caught up in an endless loop of negative stories that repeat themselves, bringing blame, criticism, or judgment. It would be really nice for us to truly reflect on how we go to sleep at night.

When you concentrate on the *Ah* syllable, it is such a skillful method. It is like single-pointed concentration that blocks your mind from going everywhere. It saves your mind from getting into its favorite self-destructive game called mental proliferation. Try to remember that *Ah* represents the Buddha mind. What can be more profound than that? If you don't know the Tibetan *Ah*, then just visualize a circle, a white circle.

Then you begin to fall asleep. There are stages in falling asleep and entering the dream state that are similar to the bardo of dying. One phenomenon that happens while you are falling asleep is called the dissolution stage. Most of the time we are not aware of this stage unless we develop a special skill or awareness. The dissolution stage happens in a much more vivid way in the bardo of dying. One of the purposes of practicing dream yoga is to become familiar with what you will go through in the dying bardo. If you can go through these phenomena with awareness while falling asleep, then you can carry awareness while you are going through the dissolution stages during the dying process. I will go into detail on the stages of dissolution in the chapter on the bardo of dying.

As you fall asleep, some kind of subtle awareness starts to emerge, a kind of knowing, "I'm dreaming." That awareness can grow stronger and be more present in your consciousness, night by night, and also day by day if you take a long nap. It may not be the same kind of alert awareness that you have right now. Right now, you are so aware of what is happening. You are so aware that you can even immediately turn your attention inward and start analyzing yourself. In the dream state, you may not have that level of alert awareness, but there will be a subtle awareness that knows you are in a dream.

Transforming Dreams

As time goes by—maybe not the first or second night—it is said that you will be able to do the second part of dream yoga, which is called transforming your dream. With the subtle awareness that knows you are dreaming, you can actually modify or transform the dream in the same way you can transform everything in life.

In some sense, you are transforming your life all the time. You are reading this book, whereas you could be doing something else today. You have extraordinary awareness in relation to what happens during the day. You intentionally transformed your day to spend time studying right now, whereas you could be going to a casino, for example, where you could gamble your money. Or you could be watching a comedy. Or you could be watching a horror movie; I hope not. Or you could be arguing with somebody right now. Or you could be doing something very conventional but very promising, like working on a computer, doing productive work for your company. But somehow you had enough awareness and intention to decide to read and study.

Also in the waking state, you have the ability to change your perceptions intentionally, if you want to. For example, imagine you are angry at someone who did something to you. Suddenly an awareness arises, and you decide to transform the anger to forgiveness. Normally in the dream state we can't do that, but in the practice of dream transformation, we can.

The texts recommend that at some point, when you have enough awareness, try to dream that you go to amazing places, such as places mentioned in the sutras. For example, go to Vulture Peak Mountain and dream that you are revisiting the historical moment when Buddha taught the great emptiness there. Or you could go to Samye Monastery in the eighth century and listen to teachings of Yeshe Tsogyal and Guru Padmasambhava. Isn't this quite amazing?

Or you could dream of doing something noble, like building lots of bridges so people can walk from one place to another. Or you could start dreaming yourself into somewhere in Oakland or Berkeley, and start feeding gourmet food to the homeless in your dream, instead of dreaming about being chased by demons and tigers, or instead of having a fist fight with somebody in your dream. This is called transforming dreams. The whole purpose is to transform our consciousness. There are two means of awakening: purification and accumulation. We accumulate good deeds and purify our unwholesome habits. We are transforming or purifying our consciousness to become more wholesome and enlightened. Even doing this in sleep has merit.

The ability to recognize a dream as a dream and then transform it should not be confused with the idea of lucid dreaming, which is very popular and seems similar. I think that people who practice dream yoga and people interested in lucid dreams might have very different intentions. We recognize dreams as dreams so we that can see the illusion of life and then engage with spiritual practice in order to evolve; in other words, so that we can be enlightened. Lucid dreaming can have a more mundane motivation to do fun things, like go to a good restaurant, take a vacation with your soulmate on an island, or who knows what else. The term "dream yoga," while it may have been co-opted to represent lucid dreaming, is a spiritual practice with a transcendent purpose and with roots in Tantric Buddhism.

When you go to bed with the last thought of something noble or wholesome, something changes in your consciousness. If you develop the intention to maintain awareness and visualize the *Ah* syllable, it is already changing your consciousness. Even if you are not able to clearly recognize a dramatic dream, the practice will influence your consciousness, most probably so that you may have more of what you could call wholesome dreams. We won't say "spiritual dreams" but wholesome dreams. Not only that, you might be able to stop repeating some old habits in your dreams, old habits that have to do with your unconscious karmic patterns.

Clear Light

The last part of dream yoga is called training to experience the dream as clear light. Clear light in Tibetan is *ösel* (W. *'od gsal*), or in Sanskrit, *prabhāsvara*. It is quite profound. This is perhaps the most important part of the dream bardo, which has to do with experiencing an undeluded state of consciousness while you are sleeping. Then it doesn't matter whether there is a dream or not. You are able to experience the pure nature of your consciousness, one that is pristine, luminous, and freed from all ordinary mental activities, while you are sleeping. You are basically in a meditative state while you are dreaming or sleeping. A Tantric text says, "Body, speech, and mind are focused intently, and the supreme state of utter lucidity blends with sleep."

The term "clear light" is found throughout Buddhist writings, and sometimes it is important to understand it in context. *Osel* itself has many subtle nuances in Tantric Buddhism. It is a profound experience—that can happen on special occasions or can be induced with methods—where one can experience the nature of reality, the nature of oneself, freed from any distortion of egoic mind. People who do Tantric Buddhist practices often have firsthand experience of *osel*. People who haven't done those practices can think it is too abstract. It is important not to reject something because it is not familiar to you. Often many of these experiences are hard to communicate to others, and sometimes people are encouraged to keep them to themselves or to share them only with their master or spiritual friend.

There is a certain set of practices that can help you experience this state of consciousness, the clear light. These practices are quite clearly described in Tantric Buddhist texts. Here, it is not necessary to go into all the details. The secret of experiencing this state is, again, setting the intention before you fall asleep. You might say, "May I have the ability to experience the clear light in the sleeping state."

By the way, do not think that experiencing clear light is something that we can figure out by simply reading some instruction on it. Perhaps it requires a great length of time in meditation practice and particularly being familiar with Tantric Buddhism. I encourage anybody who is interested in this topic to study the Dzogchen teachings. Then this can become a reality, not something abstract. One of the eighty-four Mahasiddhas, Lavapa, is said to have slept a lot, meditating on the clear light in the dream for twelve years, and then he became enlightened. This third stage of dream yoga is based on the ground of having the direct experience of nature of mind, or clear light of consciousness. Without that, perhaps this third stage of dream yoga will not really apply.

When you experience clear light, you may experience it as a free, ego-less awareness, like the primordial ground of your consciousness, completely lacking any kind of ordinary thoughts or reference points. It is said that in this experience, you feel that whatever you see in that state is vivid and clear, as if you are awake. Most importantly, you experience the nature of mind that is like the clear, blue sky with no obscuration, a sky without moon or sun. Clear light here is really the same as "nature of mind." In general, the traditional teachings say that if someone has realized nature of mind, they will go through the stages of dissolution and then remain in the nature of mind while they are sleeping. True clear light refers to the nature of mind.

Sleeping and dreaming are a big part of our life. Most people sleep six, seven, or eight hours each day. A third of our life is spent in the sleep state. Obviously, it is so important that we cannot just ignore it. Therefore, in that sense, among the many bardos we go through in our lifetime, the dream bardo is quite an important bardo. It is important to engage with this part of life as consciously as possible and integrate it with our spiritual practices, such as through practicing dream yoga.

If you can, please try to remember these teachings and use them to the best of your ability. The whole point is to wake up from delusion as soon as possible. When I decided to teach on the bardos I was motivated by one important thought— the urgency that I feel myself to become enlightened sooner. This thought has been inside of me, and out of that thought, the whole idea of offering the bardo teachings also manifested.

Therefore, let's try to really feel what Karma Lingpa said: this life is so short. No time to squander. It is also not so much fun to continue being the slave of the three poisons or five poisons. It is not really funny anymore. We have to say, "Enough is enough," to use ordinary slang. Enough is enough. It is not so much fun to get lost in the ego's game. It is so exhausting; it is also very sad.

I know it is not easy to wake up but at least let's have some urgency, a divine urgency to take everything into our heart and use this teaching to wake up. Not only is life short, but we also don't know anything about how our life will unfold. So I would like everybody to take these teachings into your heart of hearts and to go for the highest. Go for the highest, the highest level of Dharma. Don't aim for the medium level of Dharma or the lower level. Aim for the highest level of Dharma. Why not?

PART III:
BARDO OF MEDITATION

ཀྱེ་མ༔ བདག་ལ་བསམ་གཏན་བར་དོ་འཆར་དུས་འདིར༔

རྣམ་གཡེང་འཁྲུལ་པའི་ཚོགས་རྣམས་སྤངས་བྱས་ནས༔

ཡེངས་མེད་འཛིན་མེད་མཐའ་བྲལ་ངང་ལ་འཇོག༔

བསྐྱེད་རྫོགས་གཉིས་ལ་བརྟན་པ་ཐོབ་པར་བྱ༔

བྱ་བ་སྤངས་ནས་རྩེ་གཅིག་བསྒོམ་དུས་འདིར༔

ཉོན་མོངས་འཁྲུལ་པའི་དབང་དུ་མ་བཏང་ཞིག༔

Kyema! Now when the bardo of meditation appears,
I will abandon all forms of distraction and delusion,
And abide in the limitless state devoid of
distraction and grasping,
Gaining stability in the two stages: generation and completion.
During this time of practicing meditation single-heartedly,
giving up activity,
I must not fall under the power of afflictions and delusion.

BARDO OF MEDITATION

After the bardo of this life and the bardo of dream, the next or third bardo is the bardo of meditation; in Tibetan, *samten bardo* (W. *bsam gtan bar do)*.

Many traditional teachings as well as Buddhist texts, such as Tantric Buddhist texts or scriptures, do not talk about six bardos as separate bardos. Instead they often talk about only four bardos, and they include dream and meditation as part of the bardo of life. One of the reasons that they don't separate out the bardos of dream and meditation is that perhaps it is more practical and easier to remember four bardos. Also, the bardo of meditation is a bardo that not all people experience or relate to. Imagine hypothetically that there is somebody who never meditates. Then the whole bardo of meditation would be a little bit strange or even esoteric.

However, for meditators, the bardo of meditation is quite relevant. Of course, meditation is not just mindfulness, Dzogchen, Zen, or other meditation that people do formally on the meditation cushion. It can also refer to a subtle state of consciousness that can happen on its own. The heart of meditation is what we might like to call awareness. Therefore, in the Theravadin Buddhist tradition, the heart of meditation practice is mindfulness, *sati* in Pali, which also means awareness. In Dzogchen, which is the highest practice in Tibetan Buddhism, *rigpa* literally means awareness. There are different levels of awareness, but one could say that awareness is a state of our consciousness where we are not lost in our thoughts and experiences. It is possible that many people who don't practice meditation formally may experience awareness or various meditative states.

If you are a meditator or yogi, meditation is perhaps a big part of your everyday life, depending on how much time you spend practicing it formally. Meditation is a bardo that you probably experience every day. Meditation is a bardo because there is a period between when you meditate and when you don't meditate, at least if meditation is considered a more formal practice. Theoretically you could stay in awareness, in the meditative state of mind, all the time. But this would be almost impossible for anybody, because here and there, you would lose awareness through forgetfulness, get lost in your thoughts, and identify with your emotions. Meditation is interrupted in those moments, and there's a period of unawareness. Then something happens in your consciousness that reminds you to meditate. You realize that you have been lost in your mind, and you want to regain your awareness, whether you are sitting on the cushion or not. So for many people, the bardo of meditation is quite relevant.

The teachings on the bardo of meditation from the Nyingma masters are also an invitation to practice meditation in everyday life because otherwise one could lead one's life unconsciously, which happens more than we think. Of course, meditation has many forms, such as prayer, contemplation, reflection, and inquiry. If there is not any form of meditation in our life, then we could live ruled by our old habits, repeating the same cycle of deluded thoughts and neurotic emotions.

Meditation also has the connotation of being awake. Being awake means to see the truth of who we are and the nature of reality. But we should not think that meditation is strictly a religious practice, because you could be a very evolved being without having any kind of religious identity. Or sometimes you could be a very religious person but be lacking in insight and true reflection, to the extent that your religious practice becomes just another compulsion. In *No Man Is an Island*, Thomas Merton said, "Most of the world is either asleep or dead. The religious people are, for the most part, asleep. The irreligious are dead." He must have seen that the whole world is living unconsciously. Even religious practice can be a compulsion that doesn't wake you up if there is no true reflection or awareness.

Thomas Merton's statement sounds a little bit shocking, something that we don't usually think about. But Thomas Merton was not the first person to express this grievance. Even the old masters, as well as Buddha himself, had the same grievance about humanity's unawareness. Buddha said,

Seeing creatures flopping around,
Like fish in water too shallow,
So hostile to one another!
— Seeing this, I became afraid.

Here Buddha is expressing his own feeling of being distraught from seeing so much conflict in the world, which is often generated from living unconsciously. All the greed, conflict, prejudice, and misery that the world experiences each day are not because this is a terrible planet to be on or because some external force is cursing humanity. It is really a self-induced problem. Much of the whole world lives unconsciously.

Not only does meditation help bring us to an inner sanctuary of serenity and give us the ability to rise above our thoughts and emotions, it can also lead us to a profound understanding of the nature of life. This underlying truth of all things is expressed in Buddhism as the truth of impermanence, no-self, and emptiness.

People may not be aware of the high price they often pay when they lead a life that is devoid of meditation practice. For example, if you never have serenity, then there is nothing to compare your everyday life with, so it feels like being agitated or anxious is the norm. There is no warning sign or someone shouting, "Meditate, otherwise you are deluded." People can be quite comfortable most of the time without any meditation; life functions okay without deep reflection on the purpose of life. We do the daily rituals: cooking, eating, driving, and hanging out with friends. We belong to certain tribes, and we think they will be there when we go through challenges. There is a safety net for us in our community and our financial security. Everything is functioning, but we are also suffering. Suffering becomes the norm because we don't even realize it.

Our consciousness can be expanded, but we are living in a limited state of consciousness and we don't know it. This primitive state of consciousness is running our life in relationship to our self and to other people, and it is dominating all the affairs of this world. We don't even know what we are missing, like the people in Plato's example who were chained in a cave, facing the cave wall, unable to turn their heads. They could only see the shadows on the wall and they never saw the real-life activity behind them, outside the cave, that created those shadows. They believed the shadows were reality. When someone broke out of the cave and saw there was a whole world outside, the prisoners inside didn't believe him and threatened to kill him.

Buddha's first sermon was on the truth of suffering, *dukkha*, because he realized most people were unconscious of it. In order to find true freedom, we have to realize we are suffering. Otherwise, logically, we can't get free from suffering if we don't acknowledge it. Even Carl Jung said that for a patient to be better, he or she has to acknowledge that he or she has a problem. He famously said, "One does not become enlightened by imagining figures of light but by making the darkness conscious." Sometimes when people go into a long meditation retreat, they have the startling realization that they have been deluded all along. They realize they have been suffering for no reason other than living unconsciously.

At the same time, during a long retreat we also see how expansive consciousness can be, how loving and courageous our heart can be. We see the bigger picture of reality, which is often concealed to our usual consciousness. There was a famous lama, a great meditator from the Mindroling Monastery in Tibet, who lived in the city of Lhasa. At some point, he started saying every day, "I'm in heaven. I'm in Sukhavati," which is a term for Buddhist heaven, an allegory for the enlightened mind. He kept saying this all the time: "I'm in Sukhavati. How wonderful it is." When he said it, he was very serious. Some of his students thought he was losing his mind. Other students were afraid he was ready to die, because in the old days, there was a concept that when a lama was ready to die, the dakas and dakinis would invite the lama to go to Sukhavati. So his students reminded him he was in Lhasa, trying to talk him out of dying. "What are you talking about? This is Lhasa. This is not Sukhavati," they would say. But they misunderstood him. What he was saying was that he was so free from his own mind that he saw beauty and sacredness pervading the whole world. This state of expansion can come through our meditation practice.

There are ancient cultures where many people practice meditation in daily life. For example, many families in Golok, a region in Eastern Tibet, have an old tradition of meeting together before dinner. Parents, children, grandparents, old and young family members surround the clay stove or fireplace for *gong tsog* (W. *dgong tshogs*), which means evening gathering. They often chant sacred liturgies together. One chant would be the mantra of Avalokiteshvara, the archetypal Buddha of love and compassion. Many of the wonderful old practices and traditions like this are now dying, but people are still longing for something like that. People know they are missing something but they don't know what. The world, even secular cultures, needs some kind of meditation practice, which would benefit the individual as well as society as a whole.

What can we do with the concept of the bardo of meditation? There are wonderful verses on the bardo of meditation, such as those revealed by the great terton Karma Lingpa. Part of his verse, which was written in Tibetan, goes:

Now when the bardo of meditation is dawning
    upon me,
I will abandon all forms of distraction and delusion,
And rest in the infinite state that is free of distraction
    and grasping.

Basically, he invites us not only to practice meditation but
also not to get distracted when we meditate. Or not to get
distracted in general and to bring a sense of faith and
devotion when we practice meditation. He also invites us to
practice the ultimate meditation, the nondual Dharmakaya
samadhi or meditation; nonconceptual, nondual awareness,
which transcends all limitations and all reference points.

During the meditation practice, we can sometimes get
distracted. There are a lot of so-called hindrances when we
practice. Meditation is not always a smooth path. It is not
that if we just sit on the meditation cushion, then everything
is going to be okay. It doesn't really happen like that.

Sometimes you can sit on the meditation cushion for
hours and hours, and then realize that for all that time, you
have just been entertaining your mind with all kinds of
thoughts. (Of course, this is not a problem for people who
don't meditate.) You find you have been visiting many places.
You visited the past, maybe ten years in the past, then maybe
went to the future, talked to people, or did all kinds of
activities in your mind: cooking food, running around,
having an argument with somebody.

Then your alarm clock goes off, or somebody beats the
gong or rings the bell to remind you that now it is time to
end your meditation session and take a break. You realize that
you didn't meditate at all but were lost in your mind and daydreaming the entire time. Then there is a little bit of regret.

You tell yourself, "Oh, I wasted my time, but luckily I'm the only one who knows." There is a kind of painful awareness, some regret or self-embarrassment, and you feel it is good news that nobody knows.

You don't tell anyone that you have been daydreaming for the last forty-five minutes or an hour. You tell yourself, "I'm not going to waste my time when I come back to the meditation seat." You come back and try to be very mindful. You hold the intention to not waste time and to remain in awareness. Then forgetfulness sneaks into your consciousness, like a thief that steals your awareness, steals your mind. Before you know it, the same pattern happens again. It is possible that you totally lose your awareness and get caught up in your thoughts and all sorts of mental proliferation. Again somebody beats the gong or rings the bell, and you realize that meditation is over.

The point is that in the bardo of meditation, as Karma Lingpa said, we could be meditating physically, but our mind could be as mundane as always. So it is important to have the intention to meditate with awareness and clarity and not get distracted in mental activity. Remember, this is only a problem for people who meditate.

The teaching on the bardo of meditation is to make sure that we meditate, no matter what style, and to find as many times as possible every day to meditate. Not only that, when we meditate, we should try to have a very strong intention to be present and not allow ourselves to fall prey to all our old habits like forgetfulness, or to fall prey to thoughts—such as thoughts of the past and future—or our repetitive emotions.

In this context, "meditation" does not just refer to a particular form of meditation. All forms of spiritual practice can be regarded as meditation. For example, Karma Lingpa talks about the importance of practicing the two stages of Vajrayana that are known in Sanskrit as *utpatti-krama* and *sampanna-krama*, the stage of generation and the stage of completion. These practices are still very alive, especially in the Himalayan regions. In the West, many people are also practicing Vajrayana with great sincerity, under the guidance of a teacher, even though these practices are not easy for everyone to understand. The tantrikas, those who practice the Vajrayana, especially the highest Tantra Yoga, are familiar with these two stages: generation and completion. They are also a form of meditation. If you are practicing a sadhana from the Vajrayana tradition, especially the highest Tantra Yoga, or the unsurpassable Tantra *(Anutara Tantra)*, then your practice, your sadhana, is considered meditation. There are also quite a few people who practice *chod* (W. *gcod*), a powerful Tibetan Buddhist technique. Even though Anutara Tantra and chod have many forms, they are meditation. Therefore, meditation does not only refer to silent sitting. Distraction also applies to the sadhana practices. In fact, at the end of the sadhana, there is always a confession prayer, where we acknowledge that we may have been distracted during our practice.

In general, all the forms of meditation can go under the umbrellas of *shamatha* and *vipashyana*. Shamatha is calm abiding meditation. Vipashyana is direct seeing or insight meditation. Some forms of meditation need an object and effort, and other forms of meditation, such as spacious or open awareness in the Dzogchen tradition, do not require much effort. Many books have been written on these two forms of meditation, therefore an extensive explanation on them is not necessary here.

Shamata meditation is a meditation that brings calmness or serenity of the mind through a set of techniques such as concentration on a particular object like the breath, the sound of a mantra, or even sacred images. There are numerous methods for shamatha meditation. Perhaps concentration on the breath is one of the most accessible. Usually it works immediately.

In general, our mind is quite wild and mischievous, revisiting the past, anticipating the future, and making up a lot of stories. Some stories are quite fantastic, involving something exciting or bringing glory to the ego, but they can also be self-destructive so that people get really worked up. There is a humorous expression, "monkey-mind," and many people tend to smile when they hear that expression because they know it is true for them. Monkeys are cute but they are mischievous. The concentration techniques work whenever you apply them. You can apply them in a quiet environment, or in an office cubicle, or while you are on a train. Shamatha, or concentration, is an utterly simple method, yet it can really change one's state of mind from the inside. But the techniques don't have much impact unless we commit to applying them.

Vipashyana means direct seeing: seeing into the true nature of reality, seeing through the illusions. This might be seeing through the permanence of things or seeing through the illusion of a personal self. In such insight, previous notions of reality tend to fall apart. Vipashyana has different forms. Vipashyana can be done through inquiry, such as "Who am I?" Often it can be simply resting in relaxation, being the witness of whatever arises. Then a great seeing happens on its own.

There is also a belief that if we sit in the right posture, vipashyana will develop by itself. A famous saying in the Tibetan Buddhist tradition goes like this:

When the auspicious conditions arise in the body,
Realization arises in the mind.

The idea is that without struggling too much or having lofty ideas that one is meditating, simply by sitting in the right posture, whatever one is seeking—calmness, insight, awakening—will happen naturally by itself. This partly has to do with the fact that if our mind and body are not bothered by anything, then they can rest in their natural state, and meditation happens, because the natural state of our being is already enlightened. For this reason, posture is emphasized quite a lot in Dzogchen. Therefore, whenever we practice meditation, it will be beneficial to apply the traditional instructions on how to sit.

*H*INDRANCES IN MEDITATION

People have their own set of hindrances when they meditate. Some people feel a lot of anxiety when they meditate. There are also people who have a hard time meditating and staying in awareness for a while because they get lost in their thoughts. You might like to look into your own life and especially into your own spiritual practice to see what hindrances you go through in meditation. Perhaps forgetfulness, distraction, or powerful emotions. Maybe when you meditate, anger arises, or fear sneaks in. You can feel disturbed when these emotions arise, and they can even hijack you completely. You can also get really tired, bored, or sleepy.

You might try to list your own hindrances. It would be quite powerful for each of us to review the quality of our meditation and even write a mental note of the kind of hindrances that we go through when we meditate. Then the next time that you meditate, remember that mental note, and when that obstacle arises, try to stay alert. Try to make sure that you don't fall apart, and that you don't give into that obstacle.

So that this whole topic will not be just conceptual, I'll give you an example of how I overcame some of the hindrances in my own meditation practice. Sometimes when I meditate I doze off. People have different constitutions, and I tend to doze off quite a lot. I don't know what that is all about. I don't have any kind of embarrassment or shame about my constitution. I just doze off quite easily sometimes. Now and then, it can be a blessing too.

One time I led a residential meditation retreat at a lovely place in Sonoma County in Northern California. All the participants got up early each morning around six o'clock and started our first meditation session at six-thirty. In the early mornings, I sometimes dozed off. At the end of the retreat, a gentleman presented me with a beautiful poem as an expression of gratitude. The poem had at least ten or twelve verses on two pages and had something like the quality of a hymn or praise. He said quite a lot in those verses about his appreciation and gratitude for my teachings, but one verse was about his awareness that I dozed off quite a lot. He wrote that verse not as a criticism but just as an acknowledgment. He didn't have any kind of weird feeling about noticing that I was a dozing off periodically. My spiritual ego said, "You are dozing off. How can you lead the retreat?" But when I read that verse, I realized that even though I was dozing off, the retreat was still very meaningful to him. It was like divine permission for me to be okay that I was dozing off, as he praised me for teaching at the same time that he acknowledged my dozing.

At first, I didn't pay too much attention to this tendency. Eventually, I would remember that when I got up early in the morning, I had this tendency to doze off. I made a personal vow that I was going to work on it. I started using all kinds of methods not to fall asleep in the early morning during meditation practice. After a while, I got much better. Then last year I went to France to lead another residential meditation retreat. Everyone got up around six o'clock and I was having jet lag, and this was not a very good combination —my tendency to doze off and jet lag. Uh oh, bad marriage! But somehow, I figured out something. I actually didn't doze off. I was able to overcome the jet lag, and I was able to stay alert for each meditation session. That was a wonderful achievement. I don't know it should be called an achievement or not, but it was very wonderful to see that our tendencies can be broken. No matter how strongly or deeply rooted they are in our system, if we have the right intention and make a little bit of effort, we can actually break any tendencies that can be a hindrance to our meditation practice.

There are lists of hindrances to avoid during our meditation practice. The lists are very precise in the Buddhist teachings. There are, in fact, quite a few coarse as well as subtle forms of hindrances that arise in our meditation practice. You can read about them in the Pali sutras, Buddhist Tantric scriptures, and Dzogchen texts. Yet all the various hindrances can be put into two categories: in Tibetan, *jing* (W. *bying*), drowsiness, and *göd* (*rgod*), agitation. These are quite convenient categories, ones that you can easily memorize. These categories are not just some abstract philosophical categories. When you memorize them, you can use them to bring about self-knowledge or self-awareness. They are also an amazing map or mirror through which you can see your mind and your mind's tendencies. For these reasons, I recommend that all of you memorize this list: *jing*, drowsiness, and *göd*, agitation or wildness.

Drowsiness means that when you meditate, you get tired or exhausted, your mind is foggy, or you are lethargic. You are there, but you are not really there. You may be sleepy, or you are dozing off. There is no more enthusiasm, no more fire, no more spirit when you meditate. These kinds of experiences as well as many others can be labeled as drowsiness, which happens quite often. When such an obstacle occurs, our meditation is not considered very productive. Boredom can also be part of drowsiness. It often comes from misunderstanding meditation—we are looking for some special experiences, which is not really the point. Boredom means lack of interest.

Agitation means that your mind is extremely active, or you have very strong emotions, to such an extent that you can't sit, or you can't really stay in awareness. Even though your body may be in a perfect posture, your mind is everywhere. Your mind becomes like a very wild, unruly, crazy elephant or monkey. It is jumping everywhere with thoughts of the past and the future, and it has strong emotions like fantasy, fear, or anger. This is called *göd pa,* agitation. It is more than agitation, but we often translate it as agitation or wildness.

Some Buddhist teachers say that if you meditate with these two hindrances, drowsiness and agitation, you can practice meditation for years and years without any result. One time, Dzogchen master Patrul Rinpoche said that if you are meditating incorrectly, even if you meditate for seventy or eighty years, the effort would be meaningless. But he also went on to say that during his lifetime, so many people were spiritually awakened and realized the profound nature of their consciousness.

So it is a very important part of the bardo teachings, especially the bardo of meditation, to recognize these two hindrances: drowsiness and agitation. These hindrances take over our consciousness when we allow ourselves to be ruled by unawareness. Unawareness is the root of all the hindrances. Memorizing the hindrances can guide you and help you work with them.

The essential point is to recognize when drowsiness and agitation arise. If they arise, sometimes there could be a psychological factor causing them. Maybe there is a reason why you feel drowsy, why you feel tired and lethargic whenever you meditate. Have you ever had that experience? You feel really strong and alert but when you meditate, suddenly you get exhausted and tired. You get bored. You start falling asleep. Then when meditation is over, you feel very excited and blissful, ecstatic. You are very talkative. People often have that experience.

Once many years ago, I gave a talk on the campus of the university in Missoula. I invited everybody to meditate for only five minutes before my talk. After the five-minute meditation, we had a talk on some topic such as no-self. But I didn't really know what was happening energetically in that five-minute silent meditation before the talk. I didn't know whether people were enjoying it or not. There was a very long greeting line after the talk. One person in the greeting line said something like, "That five minutes of silence was the most difficult time in my life," which left a big impression on me. I didn't realize how difficult it is for some people to just sit in silence for five minutes.

For many people, sitting in silence is not that difficult. Indeed, they love sitting in silence and meditating. But this turns out not to be true for many other people. Some people have a huge internal block, and other people don't understand what you are talking about when you teach meditation, even though it is really simple. This has nothing to do with their intelligence. I think every human being is equally intelligent. People can be very intelligent, they can analyze and think, but when they hear meditation instructions, their neurological system does not respond. Just like some people have difficulty appreciating certain music, like classical music. Many of you love classical music, but some people do not like classical music, especially if they are not familiar with it. You can play beautiful music by Mozart or Beethoven to someone who never heard classical music, and they would have no idea why you love such music. They may find classical music actually strange or even disturbing. In the same way, sometimes when teachers offer guided meditations, there are people who just don't understand it. It is not because the concepts are complex —the concepts behind meditation are extremely simple. But some people don't get it. So the hindrances are not just some simple mood fluctuation. There is a deep psychological or karmic issue behind them.

A MEANS OF AWAKENING

Another important teaching on the bardo of meditation is that, according to the Dzogchen masters, meditation is considered the ultimate means of awakening. Yet meditation is not bound to a particular form. Almost every spiritual practice can be meditation as long as it has the three elements of awareness, mindfulness, and introspection. Without those elements, meditation cannot be the ultimate means for awakening. The masters say that unless you go inside, practice self-reflection, and develop awareness and wisdom, all the spiritual practices you do will not be able to wake you up.

Do you know the story about Saraha? Saraha is one of the most important masters among the eighty-four Buddhist Mahasiddhas of India. One time he and his wife were sitting together. His wife starting cooking radish curry. Then he began to meditate, and he couldn't get up from his samadhi, or meditative absorption, which lasted for twelve years. When he finally got up from that samadhi, he asked, "Where is that radish curry?" Then he said, "I had an epiphany. I want to go away from home, from this world. I want to go into solitude and practice meditation to find enlightenment." His wife said,

"What are you talking about? You can't even forget a radish curry after twelve years in meditation. You think that something is going to happen if you run away from this world and go into the mountains? All you need to do is run away from unawareness. The true solitude is your pure awareness." Of course, I'm changing the words a little, but this is the essence of a conversation in the life of Saraha. The story shows that sometimes even when we practice meditation with a lot of concentration and zeal, if some important element or profundity is lacking, then we won't really get anywhere. Maybe we will experience calmness and serenity, but we won't be able to experience liberation or cut through the root of samsara, the world of delusion and suffering.

Saraha wrote very famous dohas or songs of realization. In one of them, he said, "Meditation makes the whole world dull." Saraha, besides being a great mystic, was satirical. He was almost an iconoclast, and he was witty and courageous in pointing out the futility of the foibles of religious people. Here, he is not rejecting meditation or literally saying that meditation is making everyone dull. Meditation ultimately can wake us up spiritually and lead us to freedom. Yet Saraha is pointing out that meditation can become just a spiritual compulsion through which we might find comfort and relaxation; it can be lacking in the liberating insight that can truly set us free from delusion.

Nondual Awareness

Eventually we have to go beyond a certain kind of meditation. Single-pointed meditation such as shamatha has the power to quiet our mind, and other benefits. But this type of meditation practice is based on a lot of concentration.

Eventually we have to go into nondual awareness, a state of consciousness that can give rise to awakening, love, compassion, epiphanies, transcendence of self, and enlightenment. What is this awareness? It is unbelievably simple, unbelievably easy, and that becomes a problem. Often what is profound is overlooked because it is very subtle and too easy. As Dzogchen master Lama Mipham said, "The reason that one does not recognize the secret of consciousness is because it is too easy."

Karma Lingpa, in his verse on the bardo of meditation, said, "Rest in the infinite state of your mind that has no distraction, no grasping, no reference." He is referring to open, spacious, nondual awareness, which arises when you totally relax and just be. You do not judge your experiences, you do not try to pay attention to anything, and you do not have any kind of reference point. Yet all your senses are open, and whatever arises in the field of awareness, you do not grasp or resist. You simply relax and rest in the natural state of your mind as it is.

All the masters remind us how simple, how easy it is to experience awareness. Because it is so simple, it takes a long time for people to realize it. Our human tendency is to make things complicated and not see what is present. Some people may be able to learn a very complex subject like algebra or other mathematics, but they may have a really hard time understanding this unbelievably simple skill, this simple technique, which is already part of our innate intelligence: relax and rest in the natural state of your mind.

Another human tendency is that we think we have to make a lot of effort for something to happen when we are doing something profound. Whereas awareness meditation in Dzogchen is the opposite—it will not work through effort. It comes naturally when you let go of all your effort and ambition, and let yourself be the witness. This is why Padmasambhava said, "Many know how to build meditation, but I'm the only one who knows how to destroy meditation." There can be a lot of concepts about meditation; you are trying to get somewhere or alter your consciousness. Meditation becomes all about doing rather than non-doing. In some sense, this is the working of the egoic mind. We use methods to change our consciousness and also get attached to the transitory experiences, called *nyam* (W. *nyams*). Destroying meditation means letting go of all our methods as well as our experiences. We let go of even the slightest attempt to get somewhere or achieve some special state of consciousness. The idea is to collapse the whole thing and rest in pure awareness.

The most important aspect of this practice is to enjoy whatever arises in your awareness each and every moment. There are many metaphors and imagery that describe this effortless awareness. One image is quite ordinary. Years ago, I went to visit Muir Beach in Northern California. It was late afternoon, around sunset, and a couple was sitting under an umbrella in chairs, wearing hats, and drinking something like champagne on the beach. It was very unusual to see people drinking champagne on the beach, and I thought, "Oh, this is like effortless meditation." They were enjoying everything— the waves, the sunset, the people and dogs running around. Most likely they were not saying, "Oh, I like the waves, but I don't like the sand," or "I like this wave, but I don't like that wave." It seems they were enjoying the whole manifestation. This is not a very spiritual image, but it might work. Just like that, in this kind of meditation, you enjoy whatever arises with the attitude that all your experiences are the miraculous display of the Dharmakaya, the Buddha mind, the indescribable awareness, or the primordial mind, whatever that might be.

The wise men and women of the past often saw this human world as filled with people who were metaphorically asleep, and they felt compassion toward such a condition. People get lost in their mind and end up paying a very high price. It seems that most of our human woes come from a lack of fundamental insight or awareness. Meditation is a timeless practice that can bring about awareness and wisdom, and help us clearly see the way things are. It also helps us work with our emotions and our thoughts skillfully. This not only makes one human being more mature but also a whole society. It seems everyone has a desire to become internally mature. We admire people who are mature. But the true maturity comes from developing basic insight, awareness. Anyone who truly longs to be mature will benefit from bringing meditation and reflection into their daily life.

It seems in modern days, many people turn toward spirituality and begin to practice meditation due to some personal catastrophe or being disillusioned with life. They realize their pain was a doorway to spiritual wisdom, which is truly life-changing. But wouldn't it be nice if people in this world began to practice meditation and take on the wisdom of the spiritual teachings without waiting for some calamity to strike them? Sometimes people don't know what they are missing. Everyone's life would be much more meaningful if people embraced meditation.

PART IV:
BARDO OF DYING

ཀྱེ་མ༔ བདག་ལ་འཆི་ཁ་བར་དོ་འཆར་དུས་འདིར༔
གུན་ལ་ཆགས་སེམས་ཞེན་འཛིན་སྤངས་བྱས་ནས༔
གདམས་ངག་གསལ་བའི་ངང་ལ་མ་ཡེངས་འཇུག༔
རང་རིག་སྐྱེ་མེད་ནམ་མཁའི་དབྱིངས་སུ་འཕོ༔
འདུས་བྱས་ཤ་ཁྲག་ལུས་དང་བྲལ་ལ་ཁད༔
མི་རྟག་སྒྱུ་མ་ཡིན་པར་ཤེས་པར་བྱ༔

Kyema! Now when the bardo of dying appears,
I will abandon attachment and grasping to everything,
Enter, undistractedly, a state in which the instructions are clear,
And transfer my own awareness into the realm of unborn space;
As I am about to leave this compound body of flesh and blood,
I will realize it is a transitory illusion.

ＢARDO OF DYING

The fourth bardo is the bardo of dying, *chi khé bardo* (*'chi kha'i bar do*) in Tibetan. *Chi khé* is a Tibetan word that has the connotation of the entire dying process. Therefore, while we often translate it as either the bardo of death or the bardo of dying, the bardo of dying may be a more accurate translation.

We do have some common sense about the process of dying that people go through, especially if we have witnessed this journey, the last cycle of the human journey. Perhaps many of you have helped the dying process for somebody such as a family member or friend. It is really difficult to know what is happening in their experience when they die. But you do have some intuitive understanding about what is happening in their consciousness. Therefore, when you read the traditional teachings on the bardo of dying, they resonate with your own intuitive understanding. You may think, "Oh, those teachings are actually quite right. That's what I thought would happen when we die. I noticed this internal journey when my loved one (my father, my mother, my friend) died."

There are, of course, further bardos—the bardo of dharmata and the bardo of becoming—that will bring in other supermundane topics. Yet even those teachings are very practical. It is not that you can only apply the teachings in the context of the death process and beyond. You can apply the teachings of the six bardos while you are alive. Remember, the teachings on the bardo are like your sacred compass. The whole reason that the Buddhist masters taught about the six bardos was to show us how to be enlightened, how to be awake, and how to maintain awareness in the face of all the situations that we go through—while we are alive, while we are meditating, while we are dreaming, and while we are dying. I also sometimes humorously come up with a more contemporary version of the bardo teachings. From that point of view, there are a lot of bardos, more than six. You can have the traveling bardo, especially if you fly a lot. You left your previous destination, but you are not at the next place, so it is a bardo. You could also have the career bardo, the relationship bardo, and so on.

You can experience the bardo of dying not just when you die but also in other situations. When you lose your job, or lose something precious, it is like the dying process. When relationships end, you can experience the bardo of dying. Particularly in the modern culture, there are romantic relationships that are often more transient than traditional marriages. People break up or have a chance to remarry many times, or go through many relationships. In the modern world, this takes up a big part of many people's life. If life was an epic story, romantic relationships would be many, many chapters in it. People are talking about relationships all the time, whether they have one, they don't have one, or they are looking for one. A lot of inner poisons—insecurity, self-

hatred, resentment, fear, projections—are often stil
phenomenon.

It is like the bardo of dying when a relationshi
falls apart. Then when you seek or start formin   ..w
relationship, it is the bardo of becoming. The teachings of the
bardo are reminding you that whenever you form
relationships, don't make the same mistakes. Don't go into a
relationship out of fear or neediness, but go into it with
dignity, with wisdom. Take the relationship as a spiritual path
rather than some kind of human habit running our brains—
habits such as feeling we need to have a partner, or are filling
an inner vacuum, or dumping our unresolved emotional
baggage onto somebody. The whole idea is to take
relationship as a spiritual path to learn how to love, to forgive,
to surrender, and to own one's kleshas. This teaching isn't just
for people looking for relationships but also for people already
in them. If you have a conscious relationship, it is constantly
renewed because people are always changing and evolving, as
are the situations in life. Even while you are in a relationship,
you are entering a new relationship all the time.

Here we mention human relationships, which have their
own dying process. But there is a bardo of dying in relation to
many things. For example, these days many people have an
intuitive feeling that all of humanity is going through the
bardo of dying. We feel the world is dying, that so many
species are going extinct. This feeling is not happening to just
a few individuals who have some kind of psychic gift. Many
people feel this way. When they speak about it, they are not
having an existential paranoia. There is a good reason for their
feelings because obviously human civilization is in big
trouble, caused by various factors including most probably
our own human species.

Yet there is a way to apply the bardo teachings here as well. We can be upset, sad, and hopeless; or we can recognize this big dying, learn to be courageous, have hope, and remember the messages of the ancient ones: all things are transient. We can remember not to lose joy. This does not mean to become passive and bury one's head in the sand. If we come together as humanity, there could be many possibilities for averting this grand catastrophic scheme. We all have a moral obligation to protect the world to the best of our ability while knowing that whatever happens is not always under our control. Intrinsically everything changes or dies. We need to apply the Buddha's teaching on impermanence and look at everything from the grand scheme of all things.

Traditionally, there is a specific parameter that determines the bardo of dying, which begins from the moment one is sick with a terminal illness and continues all the way until the inner respiration ceases and the luminosity of the primordial ground shines. (This may sound esoteric but later in this book, we will explore these phenomena.) But this is a general statement because many people may not die through illness. People also die through accidents, unfortunately, or suddenly, such as from a heart attack. People may die without even knowing they have a serious health issue. Someone can be active, working in the garden, being very physical, speaking about his or her next big project, and may even have a date with someone that evening, and suddenly, before you know it, that person has died. The whole inner process they go through is a great mystery to many people. It is hard to know what happens since it seems so sudden from outside.

But many people do have the opportunity to really experience their own dying process, such as someone with cancer, which might be terminal but can go on for quite a long time. In that case, their loved ones and friends often can witness the whole process.

I've had the chance to personally work closely with several people who were dying. One of them was a very good friend of mine, Russ, who helped me learn English. He used to bring children's books and poems to me, and he asked me to read them so I could learn English. When I first met him, he wasn't very spiritual and didn't do much introspection. He led a conventional life, mostly focused on success. Later he was a practicing Buddhist. Russ was also a great mathematician.

Russ was diagnosed with terminal cancer, but he didn't like the doctors who told him he was going to die. Then he met an alternative doctor who said she could cure him, so Russ thought that doctor was much better and knew what she was doing. Russ was very attached to life and, of course, for good reasons: he was well-to-do, he didn't have much external struggle, and he enjoyed life. He loved music and good food. He had a lot of things to be attached to in this world, so the idea of death was a very frightening possibility to him. He was hoping the alternative doctor would cure him, and he was in denial for a very long time. I tried to tell him that he might listen to the first doctor who said he was going to die. But I had a hesitation about saying this because people can get very angry and upset if they are not ready to hear what you are going to say.

Russ finally came to the realization that he was going to die when he became quite weak. He accepted it, but he had a lot of fear. He tried to do his best; to leave this world being the best he could be—noble, generous, forgiving—and working with his fear. He tried his best before he died because he realized he had a short time left on this earth. He died peacefully. I was there as a witness.

Russ reminds me of the knight in the movie *The Seventh Seal*, where a young knight just back from a crusade saw Sweden ravaged by the plague. Then the knight ran into Death in the form of a spooky monk. The knight decided to play chess with Death thinking that as long as he could entertain Death, he could buy more time. This makes sense, as it reflects our own fear of death. In that movie, Death made the statement, "No one escapes me." It was a very powerful moment.

The whole process of dying can be a wonderful time to turn our attention inward, practice reflection, and let go of our unfinished business. Recently, a member of our community named Bing was coming to the end of his life. When we spoke with each other, he said, "Well, perhaps I am going to die soon. But what I want to do now is to declutter my mind." If my memory is correct, that is what he said. "I want to declutter my mind." This left a big impression on me.

In his last week of life, he took time to send a beautiful note to all his friends, saying, "It is with deep connection to you that I am writing this note of eventual farewell. I have enjoyed my life tremendously and love all the people, things, events, and Nature (animals, plants, mountains, trees) that have been in it... I would like to thank all of you who have contributed to make my life be the wonderful experience it has been. I love you all. May all beings be happy."

When he was sent home in the last weeks of his life, I visited him, and he asked for instructions "for my journey." He asked me to pray for him not to get lost in the whole dying process. I spoke a little about the unborn, which he completely understood, even though many people don't. In the ultimate sense, death is an illusion. When I shared this, he said, "Yes." He got it. We think life is impermanent, but do we get it? It is one thing to understand it, but when you point out the ineffable to people, they don't get it. It can be challenging to say that death is an illusion to someone who is dying. People might think you are being cold-hearted or too heady. But death is an illusion, our human concept. Trees are dying but they don't have concepts about it. The only reason we think we are dying is because we have this egoic identity. Death only exists in the human mind. My friend Bing and I talked about being light-hearted and not getting bogged down. On the afternoon of the day he died, he fell out of bed, and when his family picked him up, he was laughing. He said something like, "Well, it is so funny that I need to prove that I'm alive." Then a few hours later, he was peacefully gone.

The Dzogchen practice is all about being lighthearted. Dzogchen masters use the expression, *guyang lob dé* (W. *gu yangs blo bde*). *Guyang* means carefree; *lob dé* means to be happy. They developed techniques including mantra recitations and enlightened perspectives to bring about the experience of being carefree, of pure joy. One of the enlightened perspectives is viewing everything that happens in life as the miraculous play of the ineffable, the Dharmakaya, or *chö kui rol wa* (W. *chos sku'i rol pa*). Imagine that you see everything in your life as a miraculous play of the ineffable. If you can remember that, I think you will be laughing all the time. Your heart will be smiling all the time, even in the face of difficulties. Imagine that you are dying. If you remember this Dzogchen wisdom to regard even dying as the miraculous display of the Dharmakaya, then you will be able to laugh.

125

And you will be able to bring humor to dying just like my friend Bing.

I felt Bing embodied what it means to be a bodhisattva. He loved people, he helped them, he saw the goodness in others, and he was selfless. Losing him to the other world has left a hole in the community—a hole of grief. But we grieve without attachment. We are happy to have the good fortune to call him our friend. And we rejoice in his good fortune to have found the spiritual path.

Bing's lightheartedness reminds me of a story I read about three Chinese monks. You may know this story too. There were three laughing monks who used to travel from village to village in China. They were poor but full of joy. Everywhere they stopped, the monks would sit in the marketplace and laugh, and before very long everybody would join in the laughter. When one of the monks died, a huge crowd came to see the burning of his body. People began to prepare the body for the funeral pyre, but the two monks said their friend's dying wish was that his body should be left in the simple, tattered clothes that he had always worn. As the fire was lit and the clothes began to catch, loud explosions were heard. The monk had hidden firecrackers in the folds of his clothes before he died! All the people of the village as well as his fellow monks couldn't stop laughing.

This is a different way of looking at death. This story changes our perception of death as gloomy or nihilistic nothingness. Normally, the one who is going to die may have fear and a negative perception of death. The people who are left behind don't celebrate but instead mourn, wear black, or wear a veil. It is seen as cold-hearted if you celebrate. If you care, you have to be sad. The story of the three monks changes that narrative about death. The person who is dying could have such a joyous attitude toward death, which could bring acceptance and joy to the people in his or her life. People celebrate all kinds of anniversaries, such as birth, turning 80 or 100, graduating from training, school, or a monastery. Why don't we celebrate death? It is a huge part of life.

There can also be resistance when one begins to face death. Often that resistance manifests in the form of anger—indignation toward the injustice of life, feeling that life is not fair, feeling that life is mistreating us, or feeling that life is totally unreasonable, almost malevolent. One might think, "I'm not ready to die. I have a child. I haven't finished my projects. Why me?"

I worked with one man who was dying and had a child and wife. It was painful for me to see he was dying. His greatest resistance was that he had to leave his child behind, as I am sure he wanted to see his child grow and become independent. As parents, we have a protective instinct toward our children. We may feel we have failed as their guardian and caretaker if we die when they are young. It can be very painful, but in the end we have no choice but to surrender to what is. I felt this man came to this conclusion in his own way: that he had trust in the goodness of the universe, that his child would be okay, and that he could let go.

If we are stuck with anger, we can't really open our hearts and develop courage. We can't rise above the circumstances that we are struggling with. If we can dissolve our anger, then we become free inside and can rise above anything. This is also a practice we need to bring into our everyday life while we are still alive. We can get stuck in anger or resistance when facing various unwanted circumstances and then don't grow inside. No matter what the story is, there is a way that we can go through this process in the most benevolent way, if we can open our hearts and get bigger.

Some cultures have more resistance to death than other cultures, even though we all know theoretically that we are going to die. Generally, death and dying are perceived as something spooky, which makes sense from the survival point of view. Death is more than just getting old or sick. It means a total annihilation of all the glories that human beings are attached to, such as wealth, physical prowess, beauty, and more. They are all going to be annihilated. This is why death seems to be undesirable. Death also comes with the fear of entering the great unknown.

But in old Buddhist cultures, such as the Tibetan culture, people have less resistance to death due to the fact that their value system, at least so far, has been based on the practice of reflection. They are taught all the time that they are going to die, and they may meditate on their own mortality and transient existence every day. There are reflections in Buddhist monasteries that include contemplation of one's own death. People become very familiar with the idea of death, so much so that there is almost a collective notion that we are all dying, we are a bunch of dying people—healthy dying people, unhealthy dying people, dying people who are youthful, dying people with lots of wrinkles. I think this is literally how Tibetan Buddhists think.

There is an idea in the Buddhist teachings that the moment we are born, we are running very fast toward the door of *Yama Raja*, the Lord of Death. The truth is that we are all dying in some sense. Of course, we are also alive, we are breathing. We are living, and we are going to die, too, though perhaps not for a long time. Both are true. We are dying while we are also living and even thriving. The great Indian master Nagarjuna said,

> This transient life is full of many woes;
> It is even more impermanent than the bubbles in
>   a stream;
> From the exhalation to the inhalation,
> How wondrous it is that we wake up from sleep.

Here Nagarjuna is inviting us to turn our whole view upside down. Usually we think death is something strange, some kind of invasion or malevolent occurrence. Here Nagarjuna says we should be shocked that we aren't dead yet. Death is the norm, and living becomes unusual. He is teaching us another way to view life and death.

One contemplation that really gives our heart peace at the time of dying is to see that death is an organic part of life, just like birth. There is not really any difference between birth and death in the sense that they are both a natural part of life.

Some people find that death is a liberation, like a kind of natural exit from the human body, which goes through both pain and pleasure. There is an element of dropping a burden. This is expressed in a poem that twentieth-century Tibetan philosopher Gendun Choepel wrote while he was in jail. Perhaps in jail, you might find the body is a kind of burden, and there is a desire to exit from this world and merge with something greater—the formless. In his poem, he uses a simile where consciousness is the goddess who is ready to fly into free, limitless space, but one of her toes is tied to the earth by a thin thread through which she experiences all the pain and pleasure of life. He writes:

This mind is a goddess, beyond all bounds.
The homeland of this goddess is not this world,
Yet the little toe of the goddess of the mind
Is tied tightly to this body by a thread.
Then, until this thread is cut
Whatever the body feels, seems to be felt by the mind.
Whatever help or harm is done to this little toe
The goddess feels as pleasure and pain.
If the cord is cut, all is well.
Yet the whole world fears the cord's cutting.

Gendun Choepel goes on to say if the string is cut, the Goddess will merge into the ineffable. In some ways, this expresses a natural longing for death, which is not our strongest aspiration. Our strongest aspiration is to exist, to live, and to thrive. But there is a subtle longing in people too. In the ultimate sense, Gendun Choepel is trying to tell us not to wait for death as an exit from the world, but to transcend the identification with the body while living in this world. In the ultimate sense, he is expressing the longing for transcendence. Transcending identification with the body does not mean you don't care for your body and therefore treat it as extra baggage. That is not really the point. The point is not to be caught up in all the strong neuroses we have about the body. His poem also describes our fear of transcendence because we humans are so attached to what is familiar: the world, our possessions, etc. We are afraid of loosening that attachment, so we have fear of transcendence as well as fear of actual death.

Yet dying can be the most powerful season for profound spiritual awakening, especially when inquiry is incorporated into it. It can even lead to an experience of transcendence, knowing that there is no one who really dies, if one can transcend the personal self. Death exists as long as you identify with the personal self. When you see the illusion of the personal self, then there is no one who is going to die. Such realization is expressed many times in ancient spiritual liturgies when they use expressions like "unborn" or "deathless" to describe the truth of transcendence. Longchenpa, the great Dzogchen master, in his *Instructions on the Bardo*, wrote,

> At that time, remind yourself:
> "Now I am dying, but there is no need to fear."
> Examine: "What is death? Who is dying? Where does
>   dying take place?"
> Death is merely the return of borrowed elements.
> In the face of *rigpa* itself, there is no birth or death.

This experience of the deathless can be brought about through a radical shift in one's identification. If you don't identify yourself with the body anymore, if you shift your identification, then there is no more death. This transcendent truth is very subtle but in some way, we already know how to touch that truth. Sometimes awareness of this truth can be brought about through spiritual practices, especially inquiry, such as "Who am I?" or "What is the self?" If you don't identify with the personal self, there is no one who will die.

Stages of Dissolution

According to the Tantric texts, we will witness what are known as the stages of dissolution during the bardo of dying. Various Tantric systems each describe them slightly differently, therefore, it is important for us to keep our minds open and spacious. It is also true that not everyone will experience the same stages of dissolution, called *tim rim* (W. *thim rim*) in Tibetan.

It is said that our human body comes into being from the five elements—earth, water, fire, air, and space—and ultimately dissolves back into them. This view is summarized by Tsele Natsok Rangdrol in his well-known text on the bardos, *The Mirror of Mindfulness*. He wrote, "The body of a being is first formed by means of the five elements. Later, it also subsists by means of them, and finally, it perishes through their dissolution." Some similar experience of dissolution happens even while we are falling asleep but we don't usually recognize it.

What is this dissolution? In general, they describe the dissolution as the five elements collapsing successively into each other. And yet this should not be taken literally. Each of the five elements of the body has the energy or potency to support one's life. Dissolution occurs when that energy goes away. But in the traditional texts, the elements are described as "dissolving into each other." For example, when the energy of our body's earth element loses its potency to support life, it is called "the earth element dissolving into the water element."

As each of the elements dissolves, or as their energy dissolves, there are outer and inner signs. Minling Terchen Gyurme Dorje, a great Nyingma terton from the fifteenth century, describes it this way:

> When earth dissolves into water, the body's strength deteriorates. As water dissolves into fire, the mouth and nostrils dry up. As fire dissolves into wind, the body loses heat beginning from the extremities. As wind dissolves into consciousness, the flow of coarse breathing is cut. As consciousness dissolves into space, all the coming and goings of energy-mind cease. Then space dissolves into clear light…

Similarly, one is supposed to go through these dissolution stages to a certain extent every night while falling asleep, so there is a parallel between these two bardos. For example, when people fall asleep, in the beginning, they experience that their head becomes heavy. This is called the earth element dissolving into water. Then the mind becomes very dull, and there is an experience of heat rising in the forehead. This is called the dissolution of water into fire. Then the mind becomes hazy or confused. This is called the dissolution of fire into wind. Then when we completely fall asleep, the five sensory consciousnesses dissolve into mind-consciousness, which then dissolves into alaya. This is called wind dissolving into consciousness. Then we lose all remembrance and thoughts, and the mind becomes like a vast space. This is called consciousness dissolving into clear light.

It is said that people who practice dream yoga are able to see the subtle stages of dissolution while they are falling asleep. At some point, they are also able to recognize clear light. Such training helps one to recognize the dissolution stages and clear light during the bardo of dying.

Clarity, Increase, and Attainment

According to the Tantric tradition, after the dissolution of elements, the white element or semen that you obtained from your father in this lifetime descends downward from the top of the head, and as an outward sign, you perceive whiteness similar to moonlight illuminating a clear sky. The inward sign is that you experience clarity in your consciousness, and the thirty-three thoughts associated with hatred cease. This is called *nang wa* (W. *ngang wa*) or clarity.

Then the red element of blood that you obtained from your mother in this lifetime moves upward from the region of the navel. As an outward sign, you perceive redness similar to a light like a glowing sun in a clear sky. The inner sign is that you experience bliss in your consciousness, and the forty thoughts associated with desire and attachment cease. This is called increase, *che pa* (W. *mched pa*).

Then the red and white elements come together in the heart, and your consciousness enters between them. The outward sign is that of a clear sky pervaded by darkness, and the inner sign is that there is no thought in your consciousness. At this point, there is an experience of fainting, like blacking out. This is called *nyer top* (W. *nyer thob*), attainment. At that time, the seven thoughts associated with ignorance cease.

Recognizing Nature of Mind

Now this is the most important part. After you faint, then you come back to consciousness. The sacred texts can only give an analogy or simile for your experience in that moment, so you cannot take these analogies literally. They say your experience is like witnessing vast space or the sky during a clear day of autumn, which has no conditions, no clouds, no sunlight, and not even moonlight. It is totally clear—a pristine, vast, clear sky without any veils or obscurations, not even a speck of dust. You experience it as freedom from everything—freedom from the ego, freedom from the past, freedom from the future. It is total transcendence. It is not a trance-like state of consciousness. Instead the very primordial ground of who you are is revealed by itself in that moment because nothing is veiling it.

It is as if the universe presents everyone with a chance to remember who they are, to see their true nature, their original face. This is what is called in Tantric Buddhism the clear light of the primordial ground, *zhi osel* (W. *gzhi'i 'od gsal*), the unborn Dharmakaya awareness. Almost every sentient being —even insects and, of course, yogis—will have a chance to experience what is happening in that moment, that state of consciousness. In the grand scheme of all things in the universe, there is a lot of good luck, and this is one example. It doesn't matter whether someone has been a meditator or not, everybody has a chance to experience that which pervades all beings, or Buddhanature, to use a Buddhist term. The reason this can occur is because all the conditioned states of mind, all the thoughts and experiences associated with hatred, desire, and ignorance have dissolved into alaya. Not only that, alaya also dissolves for a while. In that moment, as a miraculous phenomenon, everything that obscures your true nature, your primordial nature of mind, is gone.

If you are able to recognize such a state of consciousness as the true nature of who you are, then you will be enlightened in that moment. That would be the end of sorrow, the end of suffering. This is considered the most important part of the bardo. The bardo teachings say if you are a meditator in this life, and if you already had an experience of awakening or realized the nature of mind, then it is easy for you to recognize it at this time: "Oh, this is who I am. This is the nature of my mind. This is really who I am." With that recognition, liberation happens.

One may think that this sounds so esoteric. One may think, "I'm interested in all this Tantric Buddhist wisdom, but I'm young, I'm not dying right away, so there is no need to pay attention to it. Maybe someday when I'm closer to dying, I can practice and study the teaching." But the truth is that death comes unexpectedly, which is humorously pointed out in this joke, which you may have heard. A patient goes to a doctor's office for some test results, and after waiting for a long time, finally the doctor comes in. She says, "Nice to see you again. I have both good news and bad news for you. The good news is that you have another 24 hours to live. The bad news is I forgot to tell you that yesterday."

Perhaps now all of you are familiar with the stages of dissolution, but you have the impression that it is a long process and that you have a lot of time to do things, like make a cup of coffee, or figure out which stage you are in by looking in your notebook. The texts say it all happens much faster than it sounds. It happens really fast. Some teachings say that if you recognize the clear light, you are able to stay in the nature of mind for one day. But that day is not a regular day but what they call a "samadhi day." A samadhi day means the period of samadhi or meditation that one can reside in without any interruption. So a day of samadhi is not really referring to a conventional day that has a particular time frame.

Transference (Phowa)

According to some instructions, it is said that the best time to do *phowa ('pho ba)*, transference, and *ngotred (ngo sprod)*, pointing-out instructions, is when you start experiencing the dissolution of the sensory consciousness. Others say the best time to do phowa and ngotred is after clarity, increase, and attainment, or *nang ché top* (W. *snang mched thob*), have occurred.

Phowa means transference of consciousness, and there are very complicated phowas and very simple phowas that you may eventually want to learn. Phowa is a ceremony or practice that can be done by and for oneself, or it can be done by someone else for another person who is dying. Even though the texts identify a precise time when phowa is supposed to be performed, in real life it would be very difficult to recognize those microscopic times, such as which dissolution stage a person is going through. We have to call the shots and rely on our intuition to say, "This is a good time to do phowa." If you want to do phowa for your friend or relative, you will know intuitively when to do it. If you are playing the role of a lama, or Tibetan Buddhist teacher, then often the family of the dying person will invite you to do the phowa ceremony when the person is getting close to death. It is not as if they know exactly when phowa should be performed.

Recently, the Eastern Tibetan community where I live was celebrating *Losar*, the Tibetan New Year, and I was invited to join them. There was a lot of food, people were laughing and joking, and I heard they had been dancing the entire morning. Suddenly an older man got a phone call and then said to me, "One of my Tibetan friends is dying in the hospital. Can you please go there and do phowa?" I and another lama immediately jumped into the car and went to the hospital. There, a young Tibetan man was obviously dying and was surrounded by dozens of relatives who wanted to do something. But they didn't know what to do. Our presence helped them feel some relief, as they thought that now the lamas would do phowa, which we did. Later I heard this person didn't die for a few weeks. You never really know when death will happen, but it doesn't matter. Phowa can also be done after the person has died.

The etymology of phowa is transferring someone's consciousness into the awakened mind. The true meaning of phowa is that you are helping yourself or another person to recognize the nature of mind and not get lost in this unknown journey of dying. The highest form of phowa has ngotred in it. Often phowa is just an intuitive meditation through which the person himself or herself—or the person doing phowa for someone—shoots his or her consciousness into the awakened mind through visualization. Sometimes one visualizes shooting one's consciousness into the heart of Buddha Amitabha.

In some parts of Tibet, the forty-nine days of ceremony for the dead is observed with a liturgy known as *The Peaceful and Wrathful Deities: The Profound Dharma of Self-liberated mind. (zap chö zhi tro gong pa rang dröl).* There is a phowa in that text, which the presiding master of the ceremony conducts each day for the forty-nine days.

Pointing-Out Instructions

The pointing-out instructions were described earlier in the chapter on nature of mind. The pointing-out instruction, *ngotred,* is something you can do by yourself if you are a yogi who received all the profound teachings on the six bardos, especially if you had an experience of awakening, nondual awareness, or the Dharmakaya mind. You don't need somebody who will whisper or recite the ngotred, the pointing-out instruction. But in case you need some reminders, somebody can do this for you if they are nearby. Or maybe you can do it for somebody who is dying. The pointing-out instruction, ngotred, is very similar to the meditation guidance. You say, "Now you are going through the stages. Do not be afraid. It is time to recognize the Dharmakaya mind. You may also go through the following stages of bardo..." and so forth. You can give the pointing-out instruction to the person who is going through these experiences.

While reading about the bardo of dying and the other bardos, you might think, "This is a practice I will do while I am dying." However, the teachings say that we have to prepare right now. We have to practice awareness right now. It is not that a bardo teaching is just for that stage of the bardo. The teachings all say that sooner or later you will go through these bardos, so you cannot just learn them mechanically and then apply them while you are dying. It is crucial that you practice right now with sincerity.

Therefore, it is important to practice awareness in what are called *yün tung drang mang* (W. *yun thung grangs mang*), "many times over a short period," from now on. Dzogchen master Yukhog Jadralwa said that you should remember to be in awareness at least one-hundred times a day, which is quite a lot.

But what he meant was to use the technique *yün tung drang mang* offered by Buddhist masters such as Padmasambhava, which means that every now and then, you just pause. You don't have to pause for a long time, maybe one second, or a few seconds. Just pause and step back from your experiences. Or you can say silently, "What is the state of my mind right now?" to make sure that you are not totally lost in your thoughts and emotions. Pause and step back from your experience for a few seconds and then move on. You can do that now and then, many times a day. It doesn't have to be one hundred. It can be ten, twenty, or twenty-one times. In this way, we become so grounded in the practice of awareness that we are able to be centered in it in all situations, including when we go through the dying stage and beyond.

Part V: Bardo of Dharmata

ཀྱེ་མ༔ བདག་ལ་ཆོས་ཉིད་བར་དོ་འཆར་དུས་འདིར༔
ཀུན་ལ་སྤྱངས་སྐྲག་འཇིགས་སྣང་སྤྱངས་བྱས་ནས༔
གང་ཤར་རང་སྣང་རིག་པར་ངོ་ཤེས་འཛུག༔
བར་དོའི་སྣང་ཚུལ་ཡིན་པར་ཤེས་པར་བྱ༔
དོན་ཆེན་འགགས་ལ་ཐུག་པའི་དུས་ཤིག་འོང༔
རང་སྣང་ཞི་ཁྲོའི་ཚོགས་ལ་མ་འཇིགས་ཤིག༔

Kyema! Now when the bardo of dharmatā appears,
I will abandon fear toward everything,
Recognizing whatever arises as the natural display of awareness,
Knowing it to be the appearances of this bardo.
When this momentous and crucial time comes,
I will not fear these natural manifestations,
the peaceful and wrathful deities.

Bardo of Dharmata

Now we are going to work on the fifth bardo, *chö nyi bar do* (W. *chos nyid bar do*), the bardo of dharmata. Dharmata is a Sanskrit word that refers to the nature of reality. As you may know, *dharma* here means phenomena or everything that exists, and *-ta* refers to nature or suchness, so together, *dharmata* means the nature of reality. In the traditional teachings, this is the bardo or the intermediate state where the individual experiences visions known as sound, light, and rays, or in Tibetan, *dra ö zer* (W. *sgra 'od zer*). One reason why this bardo is called the bardo of the nature of reality is because all the visions that happen are a display of the nature of reality. The true nature of reality is emptiness. It has no form, but it is not dead. There is a potency from which forms can emerge. This is why all these visions are actually expressions of emptiness. Everything dissolves when you die, but these phenomena happen on their own; we don't make them arise. They are an expression of the nature of reality.

Before going into the technical details, let's remember that we can use the bardo teachings to bring about more awareness in this life. We can use these teachings as a sacred compass, as wisdom or insight to deal with situations while we are alive. Even though these last two bardos—the bardo of dharmata and the bardo of becoming—may sound very esoteric, they are inviting us to go beyond our limited interpretations or narratives about life, the mystery of existence, and the world that is beyond the known.

The bardo teachings, especially the bardo of dharmata and the bardo of becoming, help us get out of the limited box of the scientific, materialistic narrative about who we are. I am not saying that science is totally wrong or flawed. Science is just a language, just another point of view. But there are many languages and points of view for understanding things. For example, if you talk about a flower from the eye of a poet, the language would sound so different from how a scientist would talk about it, reducing the flower to details. The Spanish poet Eduardo Galeano wrote a poem about the seemingly conflicting views of the human body. He said:

> The Church says: the body is a sin.
> Science says: the body is a machine.
> Advertising says: The body is a business.
> The Body says: I am a fiesta.

There is truth in this. This is how the body is perceived through the lens of different institutions, cultures, or schools of thought. He is also expressing a little bit of a grievance about the materialistic reductionist view of the body. He is longing for a more sacred or positive perspective on the body.

So far, the scientific, materialistic explanation of who we are and of the mystery of life is very limited and incomplete. I think life is much more profound, much more filled with mystery and wonder than we can describe through our logical mind. In the end, maybe all human language is too limited to describe the depth of life, existence, or the universe. Human language can never really describe everything completely.

Remember that in the bardo of dying, almost every sentient being will have a chance to experience *zhi osel* (W. *gzhi'i 'od gsal)*, primordial clear light, which is the ultimate truth. Everyone will have a chance to experience the pure nature of consciousness that is totally freed from all the veils, all the habits, all the *vasanas,* for a few seconds. If you are a meditator then you can experience it for longer than that.

But if somehow you haven't recognized your true nature during the bardo of dying, then the teaching on the bardo of dharmata shows how to be enlightened and how not be continuously deluded as the next bardos begin to unfold. Longchenpa writes in his *Instructions on the Bardos*:

Thereafter, clear light appearances—
    manifestations of the ground—will arise.
Sounds, lights, and colors, peaceful and wrathful
    ones filling the sky,
By recognizing all these appearances as rigpa's self-
    radiance,
You will be freed in the original state, and attain
    awakening.
It is crucial, therefore, to recognize everything as
    intrinsic radiance.
Through recognizing the essence, you will gain
    enlightenment.

According to the ancient Tantras, if one has failed to be awakened during the bardo of dying, then this further journey will unfold, which happens in one's own consciousness.

While it is said that visions happen in the bardo of dharmata, the various instructions on the bardo of dharmata are not always in sync with each other. It all depends on which text, tradition, or Tantric system you are using. For example, the New Tantra—the Tantric systems practiced by Tibetan Buddhist traditions other than Nyingma—do not say much about the three visions of sound, light, and rays. This does not mean that the instructions are contradictory, or that one is right and one is wrong. It is just that the Tantric systems and teachers often gave different teachings on the bardo of dharmata. Therefore, the order of the visions or even the descriptions of the visions differ slightly from each other.

But according to some systems, when you go through the bardo of dharmata, all these visions happen: lights, rays, and sounds. For example, five lights will appear, which are very bright. The sounds are extremely powerful, like the sound of an earthquake or a thousand thunders happening together. As the lights, rays, and five colors arise and powerful sounds happen, it is very easy for the mind to be scared and shaken. At that time, if you don't have awareness, or if somebody doesn't remind you, you immediately externalize those visions. You think they are coming from outside. You can be completely frightened by forgetting that all these experiences are just the play of your own mind. However, if you remember that all the phenomena you are experiencing are not coming from outside but are just the play of your own mind, there is already awakening, already liberation. Then you won't be bound by fear.

Even if you know they are mental phenomena, they still can be very scary. Once, a group of Buddhists who wanted to show respect and do something nice invited me and a few other lamas from Tibet to visit Disneyland. This was almost thirty years ago, and Tibet was very backward. There was no Disneyland in Tibet. On that trip, a funny thing happened. Our group of lamas went on a Disneyland ride, but one lama, who was quite old, didn't speak any English. Our friends just put him in the ride's cart, put the strap on him, and forgot to tell him exactly what would happen. The cart started flying through a galaxy with all the stars going up and down, and it was a bit frightening. When we came out, the old Tibetan lama was very challenged and said, "I'm going to leave right now." He didn't know what was happening; he didn't know if it was real or if it was just some kind of game. I felt sorry for him. He is a wonderful lama, but it must have been really frightening because he didn't know what was going on. Luckily, I was able to understand English and knew the whole thing was just some kind of a game, just like the teachings on the bardo visions tell us.

So it says that sounds, lights, and rays will happen when you go through the bardo of dharmata. If you don't remember that they are all your own experience, your own vision, then you can get very scared. You think they are all happening from outside as if they are some kind of dangerous manifestation, and you can even faint, fall apart, or want to run away.

When the bardo teachings are given in Tibet, people are invited to prepare their mind for going through this journey. Their whole practice to learn how to remember the teachings, and to be grounded and calm in the face of all these wild phenomenon. They are told that one of the most important things to do going through the bardo is to remember the words of the masters: "be calm" and "rest in the nature of mind." Wouldn't it be nice if there were some posters in the bardo that said "Keep calm and carry on," like the British government put everywhere when London was under attack during the war? It's easy to be forgetful when there is so much fear and confusion; it can be hard to remember what we know.

Therefore, do not get scared by the lights. If you are scared by a light, then you are already projecting your fear onto it, thinking that light is real, powerful, intimidating, and could destroy you. Then you can be deluded again instead of experiencing liberation. But in that moment, if you remember that none of the visions are real, that the powerful sounds, lights, and rays are not coming from outside, and that they are all a manifestation of your consciousness, then you will be liberated. You will not be shaken, and you will be able to stay grounded in your fearless awareness, full of love and courage.

If you don't recognize the visions as your own consciousness, then other apparitions and phantasmagoria will continue to arise. Sometimes the order is different according to a specific tradition and its teachings. Some say you will see wrathful deities then peaceful deities, and some say you'll experience the mandala of peaceful deities and then wrathful deities. Whatever the order, it is said the one hundred peaceful and wrathful deities will appear, in Tibetan, *zhiwa* (W. *zhi ba*), peaceful deities and *trowo* (W. *khro bo),* wrathful deities. According to the early Tantras, there are forty-two peaceful deities and fifty-eight wrathful deities, which are found in Tibetan Tantric Buddhist iconography. Thangkas, sacred paintings, and small cards, *tsakali* (W. *tsakli),* contain their images so we can become familiar with them. The *zhitro dampa rig gya* (W. *zhi khro dam pa rigs brgya),* the mandala of one hundred peaceful and wrathful deities, is mentioned particularly in the Tantric system of the Nyingma tradition. The mandalas of wrathful and peaceful deities are also taught in the other Buddhist Tantric systems.

It is said that you can be frightened by or attracted to some of them. But please do not take this literally. This is all about the display of our consciousness, which can be either very frightening or attractive. When one goes through these experiences of something truly attractive or scary, it is important to know that the mind is playing a trick on itself.

The bardo of dharmata may sound frightening to some people, but it can also sound like an adventure of consciousness that is enticing to other people. It may sound a bit like an hallucinogenic trip, which attracts many people, especially when they realize their life is stuck in one dimension, bound by the same conventions and the same reality every day. Often people want to explore their consciousness through hallucinogens, which they think of as a kind of spirituality. It is true that many people who experimented with hallucinogens had very unusual experiences that are not of this earth but of purely expanded consciousness. It shows that there is another dimension of reality that can be experienced. Personally, I have been skeptical about people using hallucinogens for transformation of consciousness because it can just be another form of indulgence. But it is also good to inquire into its impact with curiosity. Two people I knew both went to South America and did ayahuasca with shamans. They shared with me what they went through, and it was fascinating. One person shared, "When you are going through all the visions from the medicines, you have to stay connected to yourself, to the observer. Otherwise you can get lost in the visions." She said it felt just like what she had read about the bardo.

There are also people who have visions in meditation. This can happen during devotional meditations when people begin to see wrathful and peaceful deities in their mind. They see peaceful deities giving them a prophesy and telling them what to do. They may see sacred letters and syllables. And sometimes the opposite happens in meditation. People can see frightening images, and they can get deluded, not knowing the difference between reality and illusion. These transitory experiences are known as *nyam*. So while this bardo seems very esoteric, some people can relate to it through their own experiences, which opens their mind to it.

The main point that we learn from this bardo is not to reify. This reification happens all the time in our everyday life. We have strong emotions and belief systems, which can be so powerful that they rule us, and we don't know what is reality.

Think about when you love someone. You see them as a god or deity but as they say, beauty is in the eye of the beholder. When you hate someone, they look like a demon to you. Our emotional reactions to situations are out of proportion, yet we believe them. Have you ever had the experience that when you hate a person, someone reminds you, "Don't demonize them." Or if you are in love, someone tells you, "Don't deify them." The experiences of demons and gods are therefore part of our daily life as well. In English, the words "deify" and "demonize" are a subtle hint that such things have to do with our mental projections.

It is interesting that this concept also exists in the teachings of Machig Labdron, where she talked about the six gods and the six demons. She said we make some things into gods and some things into demons. Her teachings help us recognize when we do this and help us realize that it is all our projection. For example, the first gods she mentioned were the worldly gods, where everybody in the world agrees by consensus that something is good; for example, wealth is good, or fame is good. These things are just decided by us, but they are shallow, and they can turn into something inauspicious in the next moment. For example, someone might be very happy but then gets a lot of money and does something self-destructive.

Machig Labdron said fame is like an echo. It is not real. Who is famous anyway? No one is intrinsically famous. Everyone is the same but somehow society decides who is going to be famous using some weird criteria. The whole thing is a big joke. But fame can totally bind you and become a golden prison. Just like that, we think fame is good, and we think not being famous is bad. To the ego it seems like you are insignificant if you are not famous. The ego has a hard time being nobody. The human ego always wants to thrive, shine, or become somebody. This is why with collective ignorance, we think fame is good. But fame can bind you. All kinds of problems arise, as we have seen with movie stars and others.

The biography of Machig Labdron talks about her meeting with a lama named Kyoton Sonam Lama, who had been a great scholar as well as a leader of many hundreds of monks. At some point, he got disillusioned with worldly activity as well as his spiritual activity, including teaching. He was tired and exhausted with his fame. He decided to become an aimless, wandering mendicant. He was a master who found that fame and reverence from others was just a trap for the ego, especially if the ego buys into it.

According to her biography, Machig Labdron had a very profound conversation with Kyoton Sonam Lama. At that time, Machig Labdron was already a renowned scholar of the

Buddhist doctrines. The lama pointed out that her understanding was just intellectual. He told her that when she truly realized and embodied the wisdom of the teachings, she would lose all her grasping and reference points. That conversation brought about a radical shift in Machig Labdron's life. She began to read the scriptures with the idea of experiencing the texts rather than just intellectually understanding them. Then a very powerful awakening happened that changed her dramatically. Her biography says that up until that time, she had worn excellent, beautiful clothes; hung out with abbots, monks, and nuns; preferred staying in hermitages and monasteries; ate good food; and preferred praise, respect, and comfort. After her awakening, she wore anything, including beggar's clothes; began to hang out with beggars and lepers; began staying anywhere—on the streets, on the roads, in the houses of lepers. She would eat anything, even food coming from the hands of beggars, and she became carefree, even in the face of blame, criticism, and discomfort.

This is a very hard to act to follow, but it is inspiring. She realized that things that are considered favorable are not *intrinsically* good, and if we really worship them, they can bind us, so she outwardly rejected them. She was demonstrating her freedom from all these traps. Therefore, Machig Labdron basically said we should not reify or react to what we think is unfavorable. She advised us not to get attached to what we think is favorable. Bad can be changed into good and good can be changed into bad.

As human beings, our greatest challenge is our inability to recognize when reality is completely colored by our own perceptions and projections. Sometimes it is very difficult for us when we are caught up in the mind's trap to truly wake up and see the truth. Other people may see that we are kind of stuck inside, even if we are not able to see it. Sometimes we are all stuck in our own erroneous perceptions. This is how the world continues. The whole goal in Buddhism is to wake up to our projections and delusions. This is what enlightenment is. There are little delusions that we don't even know we have, and there are commonly shared, societal delusions that we all just go along with, as Machig Labdron pointed out. The problem with being lost in our mental projections is that it is not really fun. It creates unnecessary suffering for oneself and others. Sooner or later we have to be awakened, but it is not going to be easy to do.

Attraction and aversion are the two most powerful experiences for human beings, but they are not valid in themselves. They are a display of our own consciousness. If we don't realize this, we project them onto something outside ourselves and become extremely attracted or obsessed with other people. The bardo teachings train us to realize our projections, and we can apply this in our daily life. They basically say, "Remember not to be afraid of any lights, sounds, rays, or peaceful and wrathful deities. They are just coming from your own mind. The peaceful deities are only your mind's beautiful apparition..." If you realize they are just your mind, you will be liberated. If you think they are outside, you will get lost in your own experience and will be continuously confused. This is our practice in life as well.

The bardo teachings say that most probably you will encounter visions that you are familiar with in this lifetime, which makes sense. They say, for example, if you are a practitioner of the Nyingma tantra, you will probably encounter the one hundred peaceful and wrathful deities of the Nyingma tantras. You may encounter the vision of Vajrakilaya or Padmasambhava, and so forth. If you are somebody who is a practitioner of the New Tantra, maybe you will encounter the mandala of different wrathful and peaceful deities, such as Kalachakra or Chakrasambhava, and so forth. If you are practicing, let's say, a Hindu tradition, maybe Shiva will pop up and start dancing in front of you. Or Durga or Kali-ma. If you are a Christian, maybe Jesus will pop up or Mother Mary will appear.

If you aren't practicing in any of those traditions, maybe the *Star Wars* movie and Darth Vader will show up. If you haven't done any religious practice, and you have been just watching movies, when Darth Vader appears, it can be really scary. You might think, "Oh, he's going to kill me." Or if Skywalker pops up, you may think, "Oh, that's Skywalker. Please embrace me and lead me to liberation." Or you may think, "He's not real, he's just a figment of my imagination." Then you will be enlightened in that moment.

Who knows what is going to come up when you go through the whole bardo experience. I'm just making totally wild guesses. It could be even more interesting than a *Star Wars* movie. That doesn't sound too bad; it is predictable. But it can be much wilder than just reviewing a *Star Wars* movie. Maybe the presidential election would happen in the bardo. That can be very emotional. You could be totally caught up in fear, hope, and anger. Who knows what will arise? It all depends on what you are familiar with. That familiarity—your habits, and your associations in this life—will most probably reoccur and resurface in the journey of the bardo of dharmata.

FIVE BUDDHA FAMILIES, FIVE WISDOMS

One of the most important points in the bardo of dharmata is that the different lights will arise. In some systems, when the peaceful deities, especially the five Buddha families, emerge, different lights will arise as five colors associated with the five wisdoms. The five wisdoms and the five Buddha families are connected to each other. In a way, the five Buddha families are like allegorical representations of the five wisdoms. The five Buddha families are very common in the Tantric tradition, though their order in the mandala is not always the same in the different Tantric systems.

In general, the five Buddha families are:

- vajra (or diamond) family
- ratna (or jewel) family
- padma (or lotus) family
- karma (or action) family
- buddha family

There are both male (father) and female (mother) Buddhas associated with each family. According to one system, the male representation of the buddha family is Vairochana, the vajra family is Akshobhya, the ratna family is Ratnasambhava, the padma family is Amitabha, and the karma family is Amoghasiddhi. These Buddhas are not regarded as supernatural entities. Holding such belief is considered the antithesis of the whole Vajrayana system. They are merely allegorical representations of the enlightened mind and the five wisdoms. Those who practice Tantric Buddhism could have these symbolic visions not only in the bardo but even while they are alive because they are trained to visualize them.

The whole purpose of the meditation on the mandala of the five Buddha families is to help us transcend dualism and be awakened to the sense that everything is sacred. In Tantric Buddhism, the five aggregates are considered the five Buddha families. For example, form is Buddha Akshobhya, feeling is Ratnasambhava, perception is Amitabha, mental formation is Amoghasiddhi, and consciousness is Vairochana. Tantric practitioners often cultivate this meditative remembrance known as pure or sacred outlook, in which they train their minds to perceive the five aggregates in themselves and everyone else as the five Buddha families, which helps them to see that we are all sacred.

In addition, there are five female or mother Buddhas to help us awaken from any ordinary, dualistic perception of the five elements of this world and help us experience that the very nature of all existence and the universe is sacred. The practice is to associate each of the five elements with the five mother Buddhas, who are worthy of being exalted. For example, the nature of earth is the Buddha Lochana, the nature of water is Mamaki, nature of fire is Pandaravasini, air is Samayatara, and space is Dhatvishvari.

Tantric Buddhists practice visualizing the mandala of the five enlightened families and feeling utter reverence for them, even though they do not exist outside. Once they experience the sacredness of the deities, they can experience the sacredness of all things including their body, mind, skeleton, houses, buses, highways, the landfill...you name it. Everything is sacred, literally.

This is such a profound understanding of the nature of existence and the nature of reality. It is also a benevolent understanding, because it heals a lot of conflict that people carry. We long for universal sacredness because of the unspoken trauma in each of us caused by experiencing life as mechanical and lacking in spirit. There is so much division— between people and animals, men and women, nature and humans. It is my experience that we are longing for something that lifts us beyond these divisions, something that is not offered by conventional religion or science. Conventional religion may have a dualistic doctrine, one which teaches that the sacred is separate from the ordinary. Then science teaches that everything is made of molecules, which is kind of a dead end. The five Buddha families offer us a way into the experience of all-pervasive sacredness.

There are five wisdoms that are often associated with the five Buddha families, which are:

- mirror-like wisdom
- wisdom of equanimity
- wisdom of discernment
- wisdom of accomplishment
- wisdom of Dharmadhatu

Dharmadhatu means the ground of all, which refers to the undefinable, infinite ground from which everything emerges but which is not really a ground at all. Dharmadhatu is pointing out the ungraspable source and nature of all things.

The five wisdoms are not to be understood as separate from each other. Just as you describe one thing that has different aspects, you might like to think that the enlightened mind has different qualities. There is only one enlightened mind, not separate consciousnesses. Yet enlightened mind is very dynamic and has all these attributes. It is not some kind of static, one-dimensional awakening, such as only awakening to the truth of no-self. Enlightened mind has all the wholesome qualities.

In mirror-like wisdom, the mirror is used as a simile to describe the reflective aspect of mind. A mirror reflects images, but they are not real. A mirror does not grasp at what arises in it. In the same way, with mirror-like wisdom, things appear but are not solid, so there is no grasping at them. In addition, the enlightened mind is not a meditative absorption where all the appearances of the world are blocked. It is vibrant, clear, and perceives whatever exists—from the five senses to the sacred—in an unobstructed and intelligent way. Images would not appear in a mirror if it were obstructed. Enlightened mind has the quality of being like a clear mirror. There is space for everything to arise. Unobstructed mind is free, open, spacious, and nothing hinders it or gets in its way, so it can experience everything.

The wisdom of equanimity means that the enlightened mind welcomes everything equally, just as whatever image arises in the mirror is neither good nor bad. One thing is not better than another. Everything in the whole universe is perceived to be the same, to be equal. Everything has the "same taste," which is a radical realization to our egoic mind. Our egoic mind is constantly seeing everything through the lens of duality. It is always judging, accepting or rejecting, and putting everything into pigeonholes of good, bad, sacred, not sacred, repulsive, attractive, and so forth.

The third wisdom is the wisdom of discernment. Even though everything is perceived as equal, as the "same taste," it is not a hodge-podge or some big pile of mush like mashed potatoes. Enlightened mind sees everything clearly, otherwise enlightenment would not be desirable. It has the intelligence to discern, to clearly distinguish one thing from another, knowing all the characteristics of everything that exists. It sees the role each thing plays: it sees fire as fire, water as water, and it doesn't mix them all up. Discernment is an intelligence that can figure out all the complex situations in our life in the spirit of non-judgment, without aversion or anger.

The wisdom of accomplishment is the next aspect of awakened mind. Enlightenment is not some absolute rest or retirement from the world. The awakened mind doesn't just sit there with its own pure joy and freedom but is motivated to help others as an expression of love and compassion. This motivation is due to the wisdom of accomplishment. We are more motivated and more able to benefit others as this wisdom becomes part of our awakening.

The wisdom of Dharmadhatu is the aspect of enlightened mind that sees the nature of everything clearly, which is expressed as no-self, emptiness, or all-pervasive sacredness. This may be one of the most important aspects of the wisdom mind. Often the ordinary human mind does not see the nature of all things. It is often subtly or grossly deluded. In our everyday life, we have no doubt that we are seeing reality, and are under the impression that what we see is real. We think the smaller reality of events and interpersonal dramas happening each day are true. As for the bigger reality—the sense of meaning, of life, of who we are, of the absolute—our understanding of these may be deluded. Our understanding may not be based on truth itself but filtered through our own mind, our own belief systems, and our own ideology. Enlightened mind, on the other hand, clearly sees the nature of reality as it is, without superimposing any kind of interpretation upon it. This is very important because all human suffering comes from not seeing the nature of reality. Seeing it is the beginning of liberation.

The principles of the five wisdoms and five Buddha families are not purely abstract or archaic concepts. We can embody and practice them in everyday life now and not just place them on a high pedestal. The Tantric Buddhist masters taught the way to use these principles in order to enlighten oneself in each and every moment. It may appear that the five wisdoms are some kind of perfect, absolutely sublime state of consciousness that is far from our human mind. The descriptions make it sound like there is a static, unchangeable state that only utterly enlightened beings like avatars can experience. It sounds like once you are in that state, you would be in it forever. But the truth is that the model of the five wisdoms is very practical.

As human beings we are not always in the best state of consciousness, even if we are spiritual with many years of practice and meditation. Yet we are human beings and can always expect some fundamental change in ourselves. Of course, any true change does not come from pure luck. You need motivation, the intention to really change yourself. This requires honest recognition of one's own kleshas. This is also the timeless message of Buddhist teachers—we need motivation and intention to really change. Otherwise we can practice meditation mechanically, and even if Buddha is your best friend, nothing will happen. Do you know the Buddhist joke? How many Buddhists docs it take to change a lightbulb? One… but the lightbulb must want to change.

We humans are unbelievably capable of changing ourselves for the better, or we can also stay the same with all our old habits and patterns. It is up to us. Therefore, we can expect that eventually, even though we are not able to live in an absolutely enlightened state of mind all the time, we are able to bring more of the quality of the five wisdoms into our everyday life. We are able to embody the idea of the five wisdoms, which in short, means not to get caught up in our mind, to have clarity and compassion, and to have the ability to help the world. We can't stay expanded all the time, but we can transform so that the qualities of the five wisdoms are present in our everyday life.

There is a wonderful notion that it is possible to transform the five kleshas—greed, hatred, delusion, pride, and envy—into the five wisdoms. This is very positive because once we let go in the moment of experiencing any of the five poisons, there is more than just the absence of the five poisons. That would be a dead end. Instead, there is also the inspiring sense that a very beautiful or wholesome state of consciousness blossoms. The transformation happens automatically, according to Dzogchen. It says that when any of the kleshas arise, we simply need enough remembrance to look into the very nature of whatever we are experiencing. Immediately, our identification with that klesha will dissolve. We don't have to suppress, reject, or analyze it. Simply through the power of looking directly into the nature of your experience, you realize that the very nature of the five poisons is empty and has no root, no ground. Then the tight energy to indulge in that klesha dissolves.

For example, if you recognize the nature of hatred as it arises, you will naturally experience inner freedom, as well as what they call in Tantric Buddhism, self-liberation of hatred and the experience of mirror-like wisdom. This logic can be applied to all the other poisons. If you have pride, it will be self-liberated, which is not just the absence of pride but the state of consciousness awakened as the wisdom of equanimity. With the natural liberation of desire, the state of mind is awakened as the wisdom of discernment. The same logic is applied to jealousy, which awakens the wisdom of accomplishment, and ignorance, which leads to the wisdom of Dharmadhatu.

This system is useful regardless of how far you want to take it. People can really immerse themselves in this method, apply it, and work with it systematically in daily life, constantly dropping the identification with the five poisons. Each time anger arises, you can intentionally say, "Oh, this is anger; I won't be controlled by it. I want to be free from it and want to experience mirror-like wisdom." Of course, it is not like we need to become too obsessive about it, otherwise it can become a form of fanaticism. You can also just use this system in a more general way, which is about not getting deluded by external experiences. Instead, let go or transform them, and experience awakening, which is more than the absence of something but is also a sense of wholesomeness, such as joy, love, compassion. When Tibetans translated the Sanskrit word "Buddha," they used the word *sang gye* (W. *sangs rgyas)*; *sang* is awakening from delusion, *gye* is blossoming of wisdom. Our spirituality needs these two aspects, awakening and blossoming, because having only the absence of something is incomplete.

In Karma Lingpa's *bardo tu drul (W. bardo thos grol)*, there is complete guidance reminding the dying person that this is the bardo of dharmata, and when you see the lights and visions, remember they are just the mind's apparitions; remember not to externalize them. This is quite extraordinary wisdom that has a direct and practical application to our everyday life. We suffer because rather than seeing the nature of reality, our sense of reality is colored by our own fear, our own projections. Therefore, we can use these bardo teachings, such as the bardo of dharmata, to always carry awareness, stay on the ground of equanimity, stay awakened as much possible, and not let ourselves get trapped in our own projections, fears, and neurotic tendencies. This is what the bardo teachings are all about.

There are also esoteric practices that go along with this bardo, which require a specific setting and the guidance of a teacher. But in a simple form, the teachings on the bardo of dharmata can be used as practical spirituality in everyday life. Even though we are not dead, we are always in a bardo. Therefore, there is no need to wait for the big show after death where we will be tested to know if we can keep our sanity or be consumed with all the phantasmagoric experiences. We don't want to wait for that to happen to find out. The test is already happening now. The question is whether we are keeping our basic sanity right now.

A lot of things that happen in our life are like lights and rays. Peaceful and wrathful deities are happening all the time.

Things always scare us, which causes stress, anxiety, and fear, sometimes on a daily basis. Often our struggles come from our inability to respond to events in a wise way. We react by blowing everything out of proportion. Ego takes one little problem and turns it into a huge insurmountable problem. Basically, the bardo practice is to remember that often everything we are experiencing is our own projection. The practice is to not react and to stay grounded in wisdom. This is not some spiritual practice that we only do on a Sunday, for example. This is to be practiced each day as long as our life continues on earth.

As a practice, it would very helpful to have some way of setting the tone for the day, a commitment to live with more awareness rather than being bogged down with our own projections. For example, you could set an intention or make an affirmation, an individual commitment to stay grounded in wisdom. When some big tragedy happens in your life, you could say, "Oh, this is like the lights, rays, and sounds that are supposed to scare me in the bardo." Use this as a chance not to give in to fear, grasping, or panic. Then it is possible to come away with an amazing sense of peace and freedom, no matter what is going on.

PART VI:
BARDO OF BECOMING

ཀྱེ་མ༔ བདག་ལ་སྲིད་པ་བར་དོ་འཆར་དུས་འདིར༔
འདུན་པ་རྩེ་གཅིག་སེམས་ལ་བཟུང་བྱས་ནས༔
བཟང་པོ་ལས་ཀྱི་འཕྲོ་ལ་ནན་གྱིས་མ་སྦྱད༔
མངལ་སྒོ་དགག་གནས་དུ་ལྡོག་དྲན་པར་བྱ༔
སྙིང་རུས་དག་སྣང་དགོས་པའི་དུས་ཤིག་ཡིན༔
ཞིག་སེར་སྙོངས་ལ་བླ་མ་ཡབ་ཡུམ་བསྒོམ༔

Kyema! Now when the bardo of becoming appears,
I will focus my mind with single-pointed intention,
Striving for the continuation of good karma,
Block the door to rebirth, and remember to reverse
from becoming.
This is the time when perseverance and sacred perception
are needed;
Let go of jealousy, and meditate on the gurus.

BARDO OF BECOMING

The last or sixth bardo is the bardo of becoming, or *sipa bardo*, (W. *srid pa bar do*). In case one hasn't been awakened through the previous bardos, now the last bardo begins, the bardo of becoming. The early teachings of the Abhidharma only discussed one bardo, not six, referring only to this bardo, the bardo of becoming. They didn't even use the word *bardo,* but they said there was a process after you die and before you are born.

It is said that the journey is not always the same for every individual. People can go through different experiences during the bardos. Therefore, all the instructions and guidelines on the bardos are very general and may not apply to every individual case. The traditional teachings give a general map of this journey, the journey into the unknown, the journey of consciousness.

The bardo of becoming is where you will have what is called a mental body. Suddenly you feel you have a body, but this body is not a physical body, even though you feel you are able to see, hear, listen, and taste. It is said that this mental body is actually very intelligent. You can see objects at a

distance, and you can have some type of clairvoyance. You feel
you can travel for a long distance in a short period of time.
You can even go through walls. Nothing hinders your mental
body.

This mental body, of course, has a very specific meaning
in this context. But in order to make it more understandable,
we might like to find something that resembles this
phenomenon, something that is ubiquitous. As an analogy,
take the example of when you imagine you are going
somewhere. You might be working in a cubical in the office,
then you get bored, look around, and think your life is
passing by while you are doing work you never really liked.
You have to show up on time, and your boss is grumpy. Then
you stop working for two minutes; you just stop what you are
doing and imagine going to Paris or a beach in Hawaii. You
see yourself lounging on the beach or visiting the museums
and seeing the Mona Lisa. But who is going? Your body is at
work, but your mental body is traveling. And it feels real. You
are carrying a suitcase, flying, eating food. It feels like a real
body. This is a rough idea of the mental body.

It is also said that in the bardo of becoming, in this
mental body, you are somewhat restless. You are a little bit
ungrounded, and you are moving constantly, traveling
everywhere, and very nervous. Your whole being is very much
in a hurry. One of the characteristics of the mental body is
that it is very unstable. You are kind of going everywhere. The
traditional texts say that you may see other people, such as
your friends, and you may visit a lot of places that you visited
in this life.

This is a period where you begin to develop your
inclination toward the next manifestation, toward whatever
you are going to be born into. As a transmigrator, you may be

born in a particular place, time, particular loka or world, or as a particular being. Let's say you are going to be born as a human. Then maybe you are able to see a lot of humans wandering around. Or if you are going to reincarnate into an animal, then maybe you begin to see a lot of animals in your vision.

The texts also say you will see people that you are going to be born with or people you are familiar with. A lama friend of mine used to joke about this. I stayed for a time with his sangha, who did a lot of very extensive Tantric Buddhist sadhanas. They were reading these very long texts, and the page numbers were always changing. Sometimes people had to jump from one page to another page, so the chant leaders were always reminding people of this by shouting the page numbers of the text. Although the chant leader always announced the page number, people didn't hear it and would say, "Which page number did you say?" My lama friend joked that the way he would recognize his students in the bardo is that they all would be running around shouting, "What's the page number? Which page is it?"

In the Tibetan culture, many people want to know where they are going to reincarnate in the next lifetime. This becomes a big concern and often the lamas are consulted by lay people about it. But the lamas have a wise saying: "If you want to know where you are going to reincarnate next, look at your current mind." It means you don't need to consult with a wise man or prophet because simply looking at your current mind will tell you. The idea is that if your current mind is less deluded and is full of love and wisdom, you will have a better rebirth, and vice versa. It is an invitation to make sure to begin to meditate right now. We start to take care of our consciousness right now by beginning the process of karmic purification—developing awareness, love, and compassion, and shedding all our old habits—because our continuing journey will be a reflection of the state of consciousness that we are residing in now.

So it is said that you will gain a mental body in the bardo of becoming, and then you can travel, see familiar beings, and also see the species of beings that you are going to manifest into. It is also said that you will have fear and worry if you are not in a state of awareness. As a yogi, you can remember, "Oh, this is a bardo of becoming. This is not real. This whole thing is my own experience. What I'm experiencing right now is a mental body." Then you can be grounded in the understanding of the great emptiness or nature of mind and not get lost in fear and hope.

The traditional teachings say that if we didn't recognize the rays, sounds, and lights in the bardo of dharmata as the display of our own mind, then during the bardo of becoming, one is supposed to meditate on the Buddha fields (the sacred realms of the Buddhas), or practice remembrance of the sacred through recalling one's own guru in this lifetime or the deities that one has affinities with. Then it is said that we will take birth in a sublime realm or reincarnate in the human world with less karmic baggage and with noble, spiritual attributes.

The traditional texts are reminding us again and again that there is an opportunity to change or wake up even after failing. We always have another chance. If you fail in one stage, there is another. This is extremely encouraging. The door of inner freedom is not locked because of failures along the way. Since there are many periods in our daily life that can resemble the bardo, these same wise teachings can be applied as a way to navigate those periods in the wisest fashion and not get deluded.

Reincarnation and Karma

The bardo of becoming has a great deal to do with the notion of reincarnation according to the traditional teachings. The underlying principle of reincarnation has to be understood with great care. All kinds of misunderstandings can develop around this and already have. In general, the notion of reincarnation is a wonderful antidote to any draconian, rigid narrative about who we are. One narrative is creationism: we are created by some supreme being, and we don't know why he or she created us. Buddhism rejects creationism by showing logical contradictions in this narrative. Logically, it doesn't make sense—why would someone create us when life is so difficult? Why would anyone create these utterly imperfect beings with their scenarios of violence and aggression?

Another narrative is that there is no past and no future. We are just soulless mechanical robots made of flesh and bones who just kind of popped up. That doesn't seem right either. The big question is still, "Why do we exist?" So far, I haven't found any satisfying answers from scientists. They can explain what has happened but not why.

But obviously there is consciousness; we can be aware of ourselves. Maybe in the end, this consciousness is much bigger than anything else. Maybe everything is all a display of consciousness. As long as we consider consciousness the primary phenomenon, then the world of matter is the epiphenomenon. From that point of view, the notion of reincarnation makes sense, as it is a wonderful explanation for the mystery of life.

In the East, people often use the idea of reincarnation as a reason to do spiritual practice. They use it as a motivation to practice Dharma because they realize this is not the only lifetime they will have. They feel they will keep manifesting, so they don't want to carry the same baggage into the next lifetime, even if they are currently okay financially and living with the love of a community. They are not practicing because they want to be enlightened right now or to have a happier mind, though that happens too. They are practicing to benefit their next lifetime.

The idea of reincarnation is also a way through which one can understand the undeniable link of cause and effect, or karma. Reincarnation is really about the law of karma. Karma is not always action but is also a state of mind, and means that the state of mind we live in during this life will continue into the next life. But you don't have to wait for many lifetimes to see the law of karma. Karma is quite logical and is happening all the time. If you are indulging in a negative state of mind in the morning, it will perpetuate in the afternoon. If there is no breakthrough, all the negativity gets thicker and thicker, and you could act based on it and not have a positive experience. Karma totally makes sense and is something that should be considered.

Once somebody asked a Tibetan lama, "What is reincarnation?" He said, "Reincarnation is just the recycling of your bad habits." That was his reply and it makes sense. We have good habits, but we also have habits that are not always wholesome. They tend to continue in our life until we do something such as begin to practice self-inquiry. We don't want to recycle our bad habits if we have a choice, not just from one life to the next life, but even from one day to the next day, from one month to the next month. Otherwise these habits tend to form in our consciousness.

When you look deeply into your consciousness, you can see there are a lot of old habits, and there is also unfinished karma. Because everyone is going to die at some time, you might like to hold the aspiration to let go of them as much as possible before you die. If you can't relate to the notion of transmigration, at least you can have the aspiration to declutter your mind, which means letting go of your unfinished karma and your unhealthy neurotic habits. Then perhaps there will be more joy and happiness in this life.

Another wisdom behind the concept of reincarnation is acceptance. In the East, people accept it when things are difficult or bad. Sometimes we don't understand why difficult things are happening to us even though we have not done anything bad. For example, you may be a decent human being, you haven't harmed anybody as far as you know, and you are trying to do good. Then things start falling apart in your life. Your health goes down, people may attack you for no reason, or you may have a financial disaster. Then you wonder, "Why is this happening to me?" This can result in anger toward life, toward reality, or if you believe in God, toward God. It can turn someone into something like the movie character, the Grinch—pessimistic and no fun to be around. But if you could say, "It's happening due to all the immeasurable causes and conditions in the history of eternity manifesting in my life right now, because it is their time to do so," then you could have the radical, counterintuitive, yet really profound attitude to just take in the whole thing with undisturbed inner peace. Something extraordinary can grow out of the pain, such as inner maturity, enlightenment, or courage.

There was a nun who lived in India in perhaps the tenth century known as Bhikshuni Shri Lakshmi, or in Tibetan, Gelongma Palmo. She was born into an aristocratic family and later she became a nun. At some point, she got very sick with leprosy, which forced her to keep away from the world. She started doing a lot of intense spiritual practice. At one point, she sent away her attendant, who was totally devoted to her, so Gelongma Palmo could practice on her own. She told her attendant, "You must go away from me for one year and five months." During that time, Gelongma Palmo visited a temple where people started beating her, saying, "Get out; you are a leper," since lepers were hated by society at that time. Then at some point, she heard the news that her whole family had died, adding to her misfortune. She began to do the practice of Avalokiteshvara, the Buddha of compassion, meditating on love and compassion constantly. Eventually she had a vision of Avalokiteshvara as well as Tara. With that vision, she was healed.

Gelongma Palmo's story also has a lot of human emotion. For example, she allowed her attendant to return after the one-year, five-month separation. When the attendant returned, they had so much love for each other that they almost fainted into each other's arms. Then her attendant asked her, "My precious guru, while I was gone, who fed you and what kind of medicine did you take?" Gelongma Palmo said, "I was fed by Avalokiteshvara and my medicine was the mantra *Om Mani Padme Hum*." Then they both went to live at a temple with an Avalokiteshvara image and started inviting people in the village around the temple to join them and practice offerings to Avalokiteshvara. Gelongma Palmo became a lineage holder for certain Avalokiteshvara practices including a fasting practice. She turned all her hardships— being struck by leprosy, being abused by other people, and experiencing the death of her family—into a path of growth and awakening. It doesn't matter if we take the whole story literally. It reminds us that we are resilient and suffering can be a path.

In the modern world, many people misunderstand the notion of reincarnation because it is mixed up with other miscellaneous philosophy in their mind—a hodge-podge mixture of fantasies and folklore ideas. This misunderstanding is like a soup of philosophy and is not reincarnation the way Buddha taught it. In my understanding, Buddha taught reincarnation for two objectives. The first was to help us transcend the materialistic narrative about who we are. The second was to help us have a sense of conscience, knowing that our actions and our state of mind often have a cause in the past and will have an impact, either positively or negatively, in the future. This understanding will help us be in alignment with wholesome actions and thoughts.

The notion of reincarnation should be respected as sacred, and not misused to boost the ego. People like to be someone exalted. In the modern world, even ordinary people can have an ego identity that believes they used to be Cleopatra or Genghis Khan. Of course, this is an extreme, but no one likes to be ordinary. I wonder why people don't say they remember they used to be a lizard or a horse thief.

Somebody told me that a Tibetan lama was visiting the United States and a person who was supposed to be a long-time Buddhist practitioner had an interview with him. She told the lama, "I remember lots of things but could you please tell me who I was in my past life." The lama meditated for a while then said, "You were a bird." That was the lama's answer. "You were a bird." Who knows? Maybe this was something she wasn't ready to hear. It is possible that this person wanted to hear the lama say, "Oh, you were Cleopatra, the Egyptian queen." But in front of everybody the lama said she was a bird. Of course, to be a bird is kind of wonderful, especially if you are a crane or a swan. The lama was not saying we shouldn't try to figure out who we were—we are absolutely free to do that. But he was saying that we should always remember the heart of the matter, which is to use reincarnation to accept situations and recognize they are beyond our comprehension, a result of complex causes and conditions that have already taken place. It is not about trying to think we are exalted.

Often in spirituality, people have this question: "I have been practicing the Dharma, or Buddhism, or this and that. But I'm not transforming. Why is this?" The answer is always the same. It is that we are missing the point all the time. We are missing the point because we are kind of distracted with many other wonderful things, which also have truth in themselves. The Buddha said, as do all the wise men and women, in the end what enlightens us—if that is what we want—is love, compassion, and self-reflection. What enlightens us is our willingness to wake up, our willingness to see our own neurotic tendencies and let them go, to declutter our minds. This is what really awakens us.

In Buddhism, there are two truths, known as the relative truth and ultimate truth. In the ultimate truth, according to Dzogchen, no one is born, no one dies. This notion of birth and death exists partly because we are living in the matrix of duality. We believe we are a separate self. If our idea of a separate self is gone, then who is born, anyway? Who dies? With a separate self, we have the whole story that we are born in a particular time, we belong to certain groups, we identify with our gender, and so on. There is the story of life that we are constantly living, and there is death that we are anticipating. But this whole thing developed because of our identification with the ego, the personal self. Ultimately this turns out to be a mental construct.

One time King Indrabodhi met with Guru Padmasambhava. He was moved by the overwhelming presence of Padmasambhava. He asked Padmasambhava, "Who was your father? Who was your mother? What is your caste? Where is your country? What do you eat? What do you do?" Padmasambhava replied,

> My father is self-aware wisdom. My mother is the ground of all, Samantabhadri. My caste is the non-duality of space and awareness. My country is the realm of the unborn. I eat the concepts of duality. My work is to annihilate all the kleshas, the inner poisons.

He is showing that he transcended all of them. All of these things are just mental constructs: where we are from, who we belong to, who our parents are. In the ultimate sense, there is no birth and death, and no becoming.

The bardo of becoming can be applied to many other major as well as minor aspects of life. We already spoke about the bardo of relationship. It is like the bardo of dying when a relationship ends or falls apart. Then when you seek a new relationship, or you start forming a relationship, it is the bardo of becoming.

Bardos of becoming are happening all the time. When you fly overseas, the flight attendant comes around and gives out forms that you have to fill in to enter the new country. You've been up at 30,000 feet being nobody and now you have to become somebody again. You have to write your name, your address, your age, where you are going to stay and so on. I always laugh when this happens as I think of this as the bardo of becoming.

Another example is when someone goes through an identity change. One friend's daughter was transgender. At some point, she said she felt she wasn't a woman but a man. It was devastating to the parents, and they spoke to me about it. They knew their daughter, and it felt like a form of death to them. For her, it was a bardo of becoming: having the conversation with loved ones, going through medical procedures, and so on. It was an identity bardo, becoming someone else. When this happens, the bardo of becoming is such a helpful teaching, so that we learn to move through changes with love and acceptance. The bardo of becoming is about coming into existence again in the world of form, entering a new realm, a new incarnation. Changing identities or genders is like becoming a new person. Embracing the bardo teaching about entering this process with awareness, resting in the nature of mind without fear, hope, attraction, and aversion will be very helpful.

Changing careers is also a very big event for many people, sometimes in a very wonderful way, and is like a bardo of becoming. Career is not only a means of survival but can also be wrapped up in your identity. Your career can become a huge part of the persona that you show the world. The world often defines you by your career even though that is not who you are. You may notice how often in the modern and developed nations, there is an unspoken pressure that you need to have some kind of career. Often in social settings, when you meet people at dinner, or in casual settings like the grocery store, people will ask, "What do you do?" or ask for your business card. There is also a lot of judgment around career. People form assumptions based on your career about who you are, whether you are respectable or not. Yet your job is not who you are.

When we lose a job, either intentionally or un-intentionally, there is a period when we reflect on what we want. People can get very frightened. There can be a feeling of shame. But the mental mind wants to reincarnate and become something again. The bardo of becoming is the desire to become something. There is a period of time when you need to relax, not be frightened or ashamed, knowing that your career is not who you are in the big picture. Set yourself free from all the conventional traps. Part of us knows who we really are. We are none of these limitations.

Even though I am not a life coach, there are some close friends who listen to me for some reason, maybe because of my role or relationship to them as spiritual teacher or mentor. There is a middle-aged man whom I've known for quite a while. He is very intelligent and diligent. He is somebody who could have gone to Harvard University if he had wanted to and become a productive member of society, like an engineer or a professor. But somehow, he became very interested in Buddhism, humanistic studies, and Eastern philosophy. He was also a determined meditator. For a long time, when he was young and healthy, his life came with a lot of privilege and much was easy for him. Then at some point, he realized he was getting old, he wasn't going to stay young forever, and that he didn't have his act together in relation to marriage, career, old age, and the "retirement project." He hadn't even created a home. All these issues started popping up as he realized that you could be carefree when you were young, but when you reached a certain age, all the merit of youth would go out the window and life could be difficult. I encouraged him to drop the idea that being spiritual and having an ordinary job were in contradiction with each other. I encouraged him to do something with urgency. We talked about what he could do; for example, he could become a nurse, or a plumber, or a computer programmer. He said he was going to take our conversation seriously and reflect on it. He needed a few months to figure it out and was willing to go back to school if necessary. He was going to let go of the idea that he was spiritual and didn't want to have a career.

I feel he was going through the bardo of becoming because now he is looking for a job and soon will be a different person. He will be the same inside, but he will be more responsible. His daily routine will change as well, so he will be a new person from the outside. For example, if he becomes a nurse, he will have to get up, go to work, and wear a certain uniform.

The whole process he is going through is like the bardo of becoming. I hinted to him that it was the bardo of becoming and that it was important not to get lost in worry and fear. Instead it was important to be grounded, centered, knowing that everything would be okay. Life will take care of itself if we do the right thing.

ATTRACTION AND AVERSION

As we said, during this bardo there is an opening to the next manifestation, where you will experience very powerful impulses and emotions like attraction and aversion. It is said that consciousness is now ready to reincarnate in a form, at some time and place in the universe. In general, if consciousness is supposed to incarnate in the human realm, consciousness sees its next set of parents in the bardo of becoming. Consciousness also chooses the gender for the next manifestation, propelled by the fundamental impulses of attraction and aversion. You will have attraction to certain beings and aversion toward other beings when you are ready to manifest into a physical form.

Attraction and aversion are the most powerful, primal instincts of our ego, which is a natural part of this existence. They dominate our everyday life; this happens automatically. It is not possible to transcend attraction and aversion. Even in the world of physics, there is attraction and aversion, when ego is not even a part of the matrix. But on the other hand, they are also subjective, our own experience, impulses that we are born with. When we experience attraction or aversion, remember it has nothing to do with the object. It is important not to project them outside ourselves. Our mind is just doing what it always does. When forgetfulness happens, we don't realize that attraction and aversion are our own impulses and start thinking that things or people are intrinsically desirable or repulsive. But this is superimposing our own primal impulses on reality. This is so important to know because otherwise we can really suffer from our aversion and attraction. We don't want to be with what we perceive as repulsive, and we have a desire to be with that which is attractive to us, either conditions or people. This binds us. We wind up chasing that which is desirable and running away from what we don't want.

Sometimes when there is no awareness, attraction and aversion become so powerful and unbridled that attraction turns into obsession, unhealthy desire, grasping, or greed; and aversion turns into something violent and unhealthy like hatred and fear. The very root of fear and hatred is actually aversion. This happens in regard to small things in our life as well as big issues that may cause problems for a whole society. For example, the caste system is based on attraction and aversion. One caste is considered holy or exalted, and another caste is considered unwanted and untouchable. In some cultures there is racism, which is based on the same thing: impulses that are ruling us without awareness. We think some races are undesirable, which is a projection of our own mind. Every being is the same; all beings are the same as Buddha.

Attraction and aversion happen in interpersonal connections or even without any kind of underlying connection. You might see somebody on the street or standing in line, and you just don't like them. Or you may like somebody for no particular reason. Our mind makes these things up. It has nothing to do with those people. Our mind is just experiencing its own primitive impulses.

This can even happen with places in the natural world. I grew up in a culture with a lot of shamanic influences. There was one mountain that was considered the abode of some benevolent spirits. I thought that mountain was so beautiful. Every blade of grass growing on the mountain was beautiful. Then there was another mountain that was supposed to be haunted. Even though it was physically beautiful, people in the town thought it was haunted by demons. It was a beautiful mountain with a river and some lovely pine trees in a beautiful forest, five miles from my hometown. But I thought it was really ugly because I was told it was haunted. At that time, I would never say, "Oh, that is such a beautiful forest. I wish I could go there." Now, I wish I had a cabin there, with solar panels, living off the grid, and with barley fields so I could grow food.

We are also attracted and averse to circumstances and conditions, which are often intrinsically neither favorable nor unfavorable. For example, some people might think of death as frightening while spiritual people who experience transcendence might think that death is returning to the source. There are a lot of modern people who decide to lead a life of solitude. They live like hermits even if they have jobs. They love being alone. It is a perfect situation for them. Then there are people who always need relationships. If they don't have a relationship, they feel lonely or that they are missing something. They feel it is an undesirable circumstance. But desirable or undesirable circumstances are all related to who we are and how we experience those circumstances.

The bardo teachings say when you see something that you are attracted to, do not get attached to it. Realize that it is your own projection. If you see something fearful, do not be afraid of it; do not project your own judgment, fear, and aversion onto it. Instead, claim it as your own experience, your own impulse. Then liberation happens.

It is said that in the bardo of becoming, you will see many different beings, and you will have attraction toward certain beings and aversion or envy toward others. If you believe your mind in that moment and project your own envy, anger, and attraction onto others in the bardo of becoming, then you will be bound by delusion. You will continue to manifest, you will continue the journey, but the journey will again be filled with karmic tendencies. Then wherever you go, you will carry these same karmic tendencies.

But if you have the ability to be grounded in awareness, knowing aversion and attraction are just projections of your mind, then you can still continue, but you will not enter the next stage of your continuous journey with your karmic patterns. You will be able to drop a whole bag of karmic patterns. If you let go of aversion and attraction and abide in the nature of mind, in enlightened awareness, you may reincarnate with less karmic baggage.

The Vajrayana teachings recommend wonderful practices that we can do while we are alive to work with aversion and attraction, which arise during the bardo of becoming as well as in our daily life. There are three methods we can use to work with our experiences, known as renunciation, transformation, and recognition. In Tibetan, these three methods are *fang wa* (W. *spang ba*), renunciation; *gye wa* (W. *sgyur ba*), transformation; and *she pa* (W. *shes pa*), recognition.

Renunciation

Buddha himself mentioned that it is useful, to a certain extent, to apply the technique called renunciation or abandoning. This is a useful technique at a certain stage of your path. The method of abandoning is to literally suppress your kleshas because you know you can't handle them. They are so powerful that you know they may take you over. The whole path of abandoning is to either suppress them or substitute them with something more wholesome. In some Buddhist traditions, substituting the unwholesome with the wholesome is called using antidotes, such as replacing anger or hatred with love and compassion. If you are experiencing anger, you can practice compassion to push that anger away from your consciousness, at least for a time. This method works for a while, but it is limited.

Transformation

According to Vajrayana, sometimes when you meditate, you can invite your attraction, your desire, or your anger. Not only do you invite them but you actually intentionally intensify your attraction or your aversion to the highest degree. Imagine there is some kind of karmic psychic oven. Sometimes when you make food, you can turn the oven to the highest degree, like 400 or 500 degrees. So you can turn on the heat of your desire to 400 degrees, or you can turn up the heat of your envy or your anger to 400 or 500 degrees. That's very high. That sounds intense, doesn't it? Especially with anger, make sure nobody is around you. I say this humorously, but it is also said in the traditional instructions. In case the experiment doesn't go very well, you don't want anybody to be around you when you turn the heat of the anger to 500 degrees.

You intentionally intensify the klesha. This is an amazing practice. According to Vajrayana, you keep bringing up your anger, your envy, or your desire, but you do not get bound by it. Just let it arise—let desire arise, let anger arise. Invite anger, and don't react to it. Don't allow yourself to indulge in it. Just stay grounded in your awareness while you are inviting anger or some other klesha.

Then you visualize your desire or your hatred as a peaceful deity like Vajratopa or Vajrasattva, in the context of the five Buddha families, or as whatever deity you want to visualize. In that moment, you are not renouncing or suppressing your desire, your anger, your hatred, or your fear. You are allowing it to manifest to the highest degree, the highest volume of intensity, with samadhi, with awareness, while you are grounded in nondual awareness and visualizing your desire or your anger as a Tantric deity. Then while you are experiencing these impulses, these kleshas, there is no more attachment. There is no energetic pull forcing you to identify with these impulses and experiences. You are completely free, totally unbound by these powerful impulses while you are experiencing them as they are, even at their highest intensity. There is freedom while you experience them completely.

It is said that if you have the awareness to visualize your anger as a deity while it is so intensified, a huge breakthrough happens. You experience not just a temporary nyam, a transitory spiritual bliss or awakening, but a breakthrough that will leave an impact on your consciousness. From then on, you will know how to work with your anger. You will know how to transmute your anger into the sacred, or in this context, into the mirror-like wisdom. If you can stay in awareness and not react, a breakthrough happens, I promise you. I don't usually make promises. I have a little fear of promising. But this time, I must say, I promise it will work. Some extraordinary breakthrough happens where your kleshas lose the power to bind you from then on. But this has to be done in the context of the pure intention to be free, with the true desire to wake up.

This whole practice is about dancing with your kleshas when they are triggered. Just dance with them. You don't get lost in them, and you don't allow them to completely dominate you. Otherwise, you will react to whatever is happening with the kleshas. Just dance with them. It's like the show "Dancing with the Stars." Can you imagine dancing with the kleshas? Our sacred commitment is to stay on the ground of awareness and to remember the practice of Vajrayana, which is not to be ruled or governed by these forces but to stay grounded in awareness.

When you start dancing with them, even though they are kleshas, they become sacred kleshas. Picture anger, looking like Vajrasattva. Visualize that you are dancing with Vajrasattva. In the end, Vajrasattva dissolves and leaves mirror-like wisdom. Each klesha can become one of the five wisdoms. This is called transformation, which means you are transforming the kleshas into the sacred by using alchemical methods such as visualization.

Recognition

The Dzogchen tradition uses the highest method, which is called recognition. Recognition transcends the first two methods. It transcends the Tantric Buddhist method, which still requires practices like visualizations.

With Dzogchen, as anger, desire, or another klesha arises, you don't have to do anything. Simply recognize anger as it is, fear as it is, desire as it is, and don't do anything. Suddenly you will see that the very nature of desire or anger is empty and luminous. Not only that, their true nature is a source of pure awareness. Their nature is consciousness, which has no form, no color, no shape, no size, no ground, no root, and so on. It is not concrete yet it is not nothing. With that recognition, you experience *rang trul* (*rang grol*), self-liberation. It means that all your kleshas will be liberated by themselves. You don't have to do anything. You don't have to recite one single mantra. You don't have to visualize one single syllable or deity. Just recognize their true nature. With that recognition, all the kleshas, all the powerful impulses will be liberated. They will not bind you. Then eventually they dissolve without leaving behind any trace in your consciousness. This is the way Dzogchen works with these experiences.

All-pervasive Sacredness

As time goes by, we will experience attraction and aversion every day while remembering that ultimately all phenomena have the same intrinsic nature. We may experience like, dislike, perfect, imperfect, good, and bad, but these experiences have nothing to do with the nature of reality, since the nature of reality is one and the same.

We talked about same taste, *ro chig* (W. *ro gcig*) in the bardo of dharmata, in relation to the wisdom of equanimity. "Same taste" is the idea that in the realm of nonduality, all phenomena have the same flavor, the same taste. For example, if you walk around near our temple in Point Richmond in

Northern California, you will see oil refineries. Of course, they are not very good for our health and can even be detrimental. Then when you come back to the lovely temple, there are beautiful sacred images, flowers, and nice colors. It is very easy for our mind to experience attraction toward the temple and aversion toward the oil refinery. But in the ultimate truth, the sacred temple and the oil refinery are actually the same. It is not that one is more beautiful than the other. It is not that one is more sacred and more sublime than the other, even though we experience such duality. These teachings remind us that everything is the same in the ultimate sense. They all share the same intrinsic nature, which is empty and sacred.

This does not mean that in the relative truth we should like everything. Instead, just know that our aversion and attraction are only a play of our mind and have nothing to do with reality, since the nature of reality is empty. The nature of reality is sacred, divine, *dagpa rabjam* (W. *dag pa rab jam*) in Tibetan, which means all-pervasive sacredness. The most profound wisdom of Vajrayana is to see that everything is the same, and the nature of everything is sacred.

To practice this sacred outlook, sometimes we use visualizations. Every time there is a break during a Tantric Buddhist retreat, especially in the Nyingma tradition, we chant a verse that reminds us to see every form that appears in our awareness as sacred, as a form of a mandala. You can literally visualize all the buildings and bridges as a mandala. You can visualize all the people or even animals as deities, peaceful Buddhas, or herukas. Then you can literally try to hear or imagine all the sounds as mantras, sacred sounds. And you can embrace all the thoughts and all the sensations that arise in your awareness as a play of primordial wisdom.

The idea of nonduality, the same flavor, is such profound wisdom. It is the most liberating wisdom that you can experience, even though in the relative truth, you will still have preferences. If you go to a restaurant, of course you would read the menu. You wouldn't say, "It's all the same taste. Just give me anything." It is not like you have to completely let go of your preferences.

In the ultimate sense, these teachings are reminding us that everything is equally divine, equally sacred, and equally empty. We are allowed to experience and even carry all our aversions and attractions. This is how life continues. But we no longer truly believe in the validity of our own experiences, knowing that all the dualities—good or bad, attractive or not attractive, beautiful or ugly, interesting or not interesting— have nothing to do with the nature of reality, since the nature of reality is empty and all-pervasive sacredness. All the dualities we witness are just a play of our own consciousness. This is all we need to remember, all the time. This is our practice, and this practice will liberate us.

The bardo of becoming is often associated with samsara. Traditionally, it is the idea that you are continuously returning to the realm of samsara unconsciously, with all your habits and karmic habits. You *become* something in the realm of samsara. Samsara means the vicious circle of delusion and suffering. And yet Buddhism also teaches that you can reincarnate consciously, with awareness and with a noble intention. You could have an intention not just to become something but to take incarnation with the intention to practice the path of love and wisdom. You could have the intention to become a source of benefit to the world, not from an egoic motive but from an altruistic place. They say the bodhisattvas and Mahasiddhas continue to reincarnate not out of their old habits but consciously, with the intention to continue the spiritual path and to benefit the world.

Even in this life, you'll find there are certain periods in your everyday life where you become more unconscious, get more lost and stuck in old habits, whatever they are. It can be a place, a time, a certain activity, or a certain behavior. For example, maybe you have noticed that when you meet a certain person, you always get agitated. You know your neurosis can be triggered by certain people you meet. Or there are periods in your life when you do things unconsciously. Maybe at dinner time, you tend to be more argumentative. Holidays are another example. You may live unconsciously at that time because there is so much in the air. You are supposed to celebrate and eat, yet you may become lazy and lose awareness. Or you lose your cool at parties and behave in certain ways. There are also places you visit where you may become more unconscious or reactive. For example, when people go back to their parents' home, all their childhood experiences come up.

It is good to go through these situations in your mind and make a mental note. Then when those times arise, you can take them as a bardo of becoming, and remind yourself that you are descending into samsara. You can make an effort to stay grounded in the nature of mind so you don't repeat the same old tendency. Every time you enter a certain place or specific time, or you meet someone, you can say, "This is a bardo of becoming. I know what will happen. This time I will not repeat the same pattern." Otherwise you are descending and entering the same samsara.

When you know you are going into samsara in your daily life, you can go through the whole thing with awareness and not repeat old patterns. The bardo of becoming teaches us to have the highest aspiration—love, bodhicitta, awakened heart—and to not get lost in attraction and aversion. The next time something arises, tell yourself, "This is the bardo of becoming." Then change the pattern.

After the Journey

འཆི་བ་འོང་སྙོམས་མེད་པའི་བློ་རིང་པོ༔

དོན་མེད་ཚེ་འདིའི་བྱ་བ་བསྒྲུབས་བསྒྲུབས་ནས༔

ད་རེས་སྟོང་ལོག་བྱས་ན་ཤིན་ཏུ་འཁྲུལ༔

དགོས་དོ་ཤེས་པ་དམ་པའི་ལྷ་ཆོས་ཡིན༔

ད་ལྟ་ཉིད་དུ་ལྟ་ཆོས་མི་བྱེད་དམ༔

གྲུབ་ཆེན་བླ་མའི་ཞལ་ནས་འདི་སྐད་གསུངས༔

བླ་མའི་གདམས་ངག་སེམས་ལ་མ་བཞག་ན༔

རང་གིས་རང་ཉིད་བསླུ་བར་མི་འགྱུར་རམ༔

With mind far off and no thought of impending death,
Performing the meaningless activities of this life,
To return empty-handed now would be utterly deluded;
Recognize what is needed: the sacred Dharma,
Why not practice it now, at this very moment?
The great accomplished gurus have said:
If you do not keep in mind your teacher's instructions
Are you not deceiving yourself?

SACRED CEREMONY

There are particular ceremonies and practices that can be done while someone is dying as well as after someone is deceased. Naturally we human beings are very different from other animals. For humans, there is a sense of incompletion unless a ceremony or ritual is performed to honor the one who is deceased. Otherwise, we feel that our responsibility to say farewell to the deceased one was inadequate. From that point of view, the ceremony is not done just for the one who is deceased but also for our own conscience.

Ceremony also helps us with the process of grieving. Grief is a wonderful experience, but it is sometimes possible to be stuck in grief. We don't want to get lost in grief but instead to grieve consciously and then let go. Sometimes we may realize that our heart is almost clogged. Then we have an inner assignment to open our heart and to allow ourselves to experience grief. One person I knew lost her son, which must have been very painful for her. She used to come to my meditation retreats, and she told me that one of the reasons she came to the retreats was to work with me. She said, "Hopefully you can tell me where my son is right now, where he has been reborn. Could you help me find the location or family where he is now born?" She said that her son died a long time ago. Then I told her, "This is not something I can do for you. I don't have the knowledge to tell you where your son is born." Finally, she stopped coming to my meditation retreats because I couldn't offer what she was searching for. This is an example of how we can get lost in grief to the extent that we don't see anything else, even when life is full of miracles and possibilities. That kind of grief becomes an inner hindrance that blocks your consciousness. Then you will always be living in the pain and sorrow of the past, unable to open your heart and have a meaningful, compassion-based connection with the world and with people, unable to go out and do something that is truly meaningful for humanity. If you are lost in grief, then your ability to love, to be compassionate, or to be creative could be totally frozen. This is why sooner or later you might like to say to yourself, "This is a time to move on," and let go of the grief.

Other times we may realize we haven't grieved a loss because it was too painful, and we are afraid of going through the whole grieving process. You may have heard me share this story. One time my family had a dog, and when he died, I didn't feel grief. But many years after that, one day I was flying in an airplane. Somehow this dog kept coming back to my mind. Then I felt a very powerful grief, one that I never felt before, and I wrote a poem as a way to honor that dog. It was such a powerful grief that I almost started sobbing. I looked around the plane because I didn't want to cry in front of all the people. I learned later that when you fly in an airplane you can be very sentimental and emotional. Something happens to your brain at the higher altitude. Research has discovered that people are very vulnerable and sensitive when they fly at a high altitude, and they often cry or laugh. Maybe my experience had something to do with that. In any case, I felt a powerful grief, and I started sobbing inwardly as I finished the poem to honor the dog. When I came back home, I even did a little ceremony for that dog. It felt very good because somehow, without that grief, there was a place in my heart that was frozen in some sense. When I experienced that grief, it was not only that I was grieving over the loss of this dog, but I felt it helped me to open my heart one more time. Once our heart is open, we are much more capable of experiencing courage, compassion, and loving-kindness.

A ceremony is a way for us to grieve and then open our hearts and let go. Even very secular communities who are not officially associated with a religion offer sacred ceremonies on special occasions such as death, when a funeral ceremony is often held. In Japan, which today is an extremely secular country, most young people don't have any religious identity. At the same time, they might invite a Shinto priest to bless their child when it is born, hold a Christian ceremony for a wedding, and then invite a Buddhist priest to conduct a funeral ceremony. Other than that, their everyday life may be secular, with no formal religious practice.

These days, for people who are more or less connected with a tradition, there are ceremonies that can be conducted by people themselves or by someone who is asked to perform it. For example, in the East—in Tibet or other Buddhist countries—people offer *dana*, or a financial donation, for someone to perform ceremonies and prayers for their deceased loved ones. In modern cultures, people may compose their own ceremony by infusing some traditional practices with their own inventions or inspiration. In general, it seems that human beings are very deeply in need of ceremony. It is possible this could change some day, but so far, this is what is happening.

Within Tibetan Buddhist cultures, the ceremonies for the dead differ based on the particular lineage, such as the two lineages of Geluk and Nyingma. Often when someone dies in a Geluk community, a group of monks and nuns will come and recite liturgies for one day. In the Nyingma community, the family will sponsor a group of monks or nuns for forty-nine days starting from the time of the death of their beloved. The group will rotate their roles and perform the ceremony known as *zhi tro* (W. *zhi khro*), which belongs to the same cycle of teachings as the *bardo tu drul* (W. *bardo thos grol*) from Karma Lingpa.

For Tibetan people, the family bond is extremely strong. They are extremely attached, they tend to help each other, and they also share their sorrow and happiness. Because of the strong family bond, when someone dies, there is a lot of emotional grief, even while there is an acceptance that comes from the Buddhist concepts of impermanence. When the monks and nuns come to the ceremony, often the family will feel emotionally supported by them and are very thankful. A sacred bond is created between the family and the monks and nuns who do the ceremony.

When I was young, many families in Eastern Tibet invited me to do the *zhi tro* ceremony. Sometimes people from different villages would send a horse to bring me to another village, where I would stay for seven days. Other monks would come as well. We would do the ceremony all day but during the breaks, we would have time for exciting philosophical conversations, and we would learn a lot. The older ones would tell us the stories of the past. For us, it was more than just doing a ceremony. It was learning, making acquaintances, and creating friendship. Then when we returned home, the family would send us with a whole bag of food, especially oil-fried bread, to bring to our home.

During the ceremony, there would be a *tsen jang* (W. *mtshan byang*), which is an image of a person on a piece of paper attached to a stick. The stick would be pushed into a clay holder with a beautiful design. Above the image was a tiny umbrella. The image represented the person who died. During the ceremony, the presiding master would offer prayers to the image as if it were the deceased person. After forty-nine days, the image would be burned. It is very possible that these practices may be dying now.

Those ceremonies were more than just a ceremony. At that time, I didn't know this very well. Later I realized that the *zhi tro* ceremony was and is a profound liturgy that captures the very depth of Buddhism. I spent many days doing those ceremonies, and sometimes I would have the thought, "I should be practicing meditation or studying a Buddhist text at a monastery." I had this kind of regret. Later I realized doing those ceremonies was as profound as all the other things I wished to do. Even today, I feel that a lot of things that I know came from conducting those ceremonies. These ceremonies rest on a very nondual philosophy. Outwardly people would not know their true meaning because they have so many forms including what is called exorcism. But the exorcism is really about exorcising the ego rather than any kind of demonic forces. The whole thing is a very elaborate Tantric Buddhist liturgy that is a form of practice where you can meditate on the nature of mind.

Today, in many developed countries, since all the sacred traditions are dying, there are not so many people who have the profession to do these ceremonies. At the same time, as an individual, you can offer your own ceremonies for the deceased, especially when it is someone you know well, such as a friend or relative.

Quite often, many Western Buddhists ask me what kind of ceremony they should do when someone dies. The whole ceremony doesn't have to be long, lengthy, or complicated. Usually I suggest they light a candle and recite prayers that they already know, then dedicate the entire spiritual practice to the person who passed away.

There are three mantras that anyone can chant for the deceased one, whether the person was Buddhist or not. One mantra is the six-syllable mantra of Avalokiteshvara, which is *Om Mani Padme Hum*. Avalokiteshvara is the archetypal Buddha who signifies boundless love. The meaning of the mantra is to pray that all beings be free from the prison of the six internal afflictions: pride, envy, attachment, ignorance, greed, and hatred. It is an invitation to experience the true nature of one's consciousness, which is free from these inner poisons.

Another mantra is the mantra of Tara. Tara is a female archetypal Buddha who represents all-embracing compassion. Her mantra is *Om Taré Tutaré Turé Swaha*. This mantra is also a prayer to be free from the eight dangers, which are metaphorical representations of eight kinds of kleshas, such as attachment, wrong views, pride, jealousy, hatred, doubt or confusion, greed, and ignorance. By offering the mantra, we are praying that the consciousness of the deceased one as well as everyone else will be protected from these eight dangers.

The third mantra we can use is *Ah Aah Sha Sa Mah Ha*, which is considered the most profound mantra according to the Nyingma tradition. It is a random selection of Sanskrit syllables and has no conceptual meaning, yet it points directly to nature of mind. This can be chanted by anybody, with the intention that the deceased one is in the most benevolent conditions possible.

A ceremony could be done every day for forty-nine days. It can be done with a lamp or candle lit in front of a personal altar where sacred images have been placed. Sometimes you can have a picture of the deceased one placed nearby, and you chant the mantras in front of their image.

If you are chanting mantras or a liturgy, you already have directions about what kinds of thoughts or intentions you should hold. You can also can improvise and do your own prayer, something that seems to be right in your own heart. For example, "May you find peace. May you find clarity. May you not be lost in confusion or fear." You could say "May you become liberated, awakened in primordial purity," especially if you are a Buddhist practicing Dzogchen. If you are following another religion, you can do prayers in your own tradition.

The whole point of the ceremony is to honor the dead. When we feel we have honored them, then our duty is complete, and we can say the final farewell. We did what we needed to do on our part. The ceremony can help us as well, especially if it is for someone close to us. It can resolve unfinished issues and offer another chance to show our utmost love to that person.

In the end, let's remember how beautiful this human life is. When one is struck by sorrow, life feels too long—but when joy bursts forth, life feels too short, like watching a sunset that will dissolve at any moment. Now and then, when our mind is in the right state, life becomes unbearably beautiful. You may be sitting with your loved ones, perhaps classical music is playing,—maybe some music from Swan Lake—clouds are drifting in the valley, a candle is burning on the table as if a spirit is dancing. Then one may feel how precious and beautiful this human life can be. Regardless of the situations we go through, if our heart is courageous enough to open, the beauty of life can be found in almost any moment. Even death is part of that beauty, whether it is one's own death or the death of a loved one. Death is not separate from life but is part of life. Knowing this, everything—birth and death—can be embraced by our heart.

DEDICATION

I hope that you remember these teachings and apply them in everyday life, in order to learn how to maintain your awareness, and how to be enlightened as much as possible through all the different events of your life, whatever you may go through. We are always going through something.

The six bardos completely cover all the events in our life, from morning to night, and from night all the way to morning, including the dreaming and sleeping states. They include all the important periods that we experience—illness, old age, relationships, separation, death, and dying. The bardos are even the countless periods during our day, such as meditation, post-meditation, lunch, the afternoon, taking a nap, driving a car on the highway, and so on. They encompass all the major periods as well as the countless minor periods. Remember there are more than six bardos, as we already mentioned. I think we could say there is a relationship bardo, career bardo, traveling bardo, eating bardo, taking a nap bardo, and so many more: driving bardo, rush-hour bardo, taking a shower bardo, brushing your teeth bardo, cooking bardo, laundry bardo... There are countless bardos we can come up with.

The bardo teachings invite us to always stay in awareness, all the time, regardless of what bardo we are going through. The whole point is not to be lost in unawareness but to remember to always stay grounded in awareness, the Buddha mind, the nondual, egoless awareness.

Let's dedicate the merit, the *punya*, the blessings of these bardo teachings as a source of awakening and liberation to all beings who are wandering in samsara. May every being be awakened to their true nature as the Dharmakaya and find everlasting bliss, joy, and freedom.

ABOUT THE AUTHOR

Anam Thubten grew up in Tibet and at an early age began to practice in the Nyingma tradition of Tibetan Buddhism. He is the founder and spiritual advisor of Dharmata Foundation and teaches widely in the United States and abroad. Anam Thubten's published books in English include *No Self, No Problem*; *The Magic of Awareness*; *Embracing Each Moment: A Guide to the Awakened Life*; and *Fragrance of Emptiness: A Commentary on the Heart Sutra*. More information about Anam Thubten, including his teaching calendar, can be found online at dharmata.org.

CPSIA information can be obtained
at www.ICGtesting.com
Printed in the USA
LVHW052049030723
751451LV00004B/364

9 781732 020825